Fantastic Four
DOOM

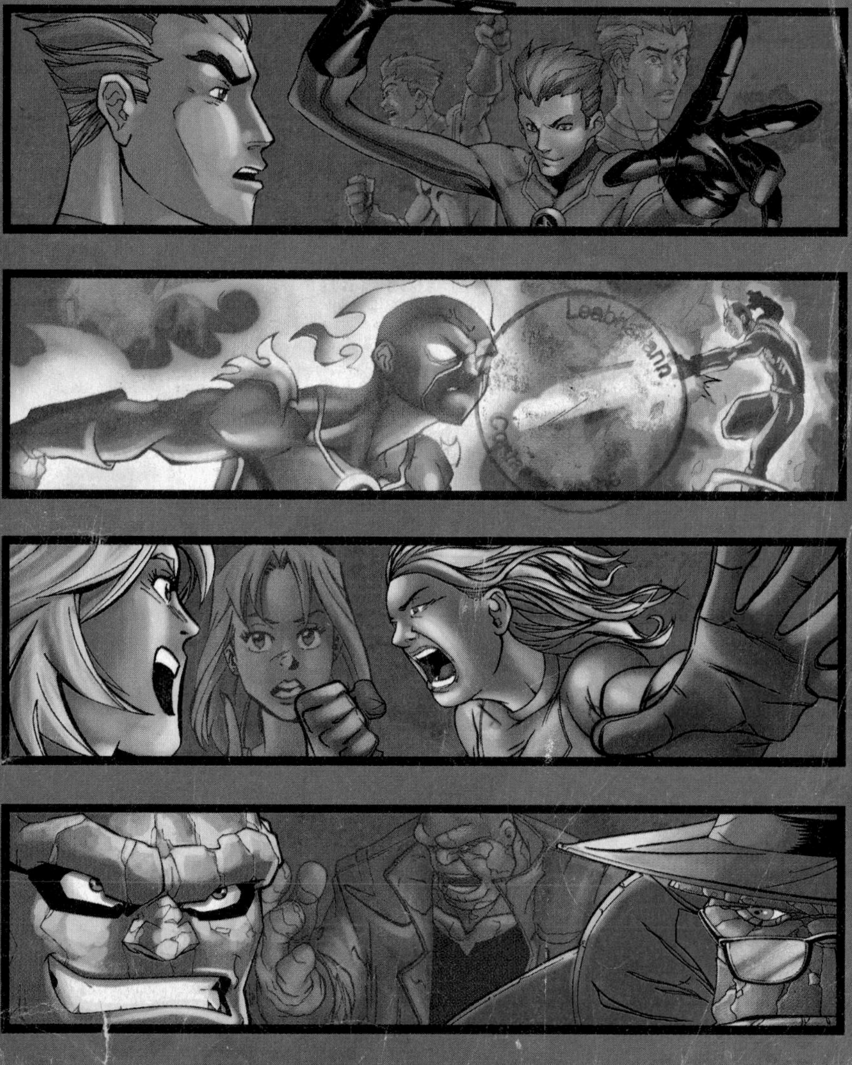

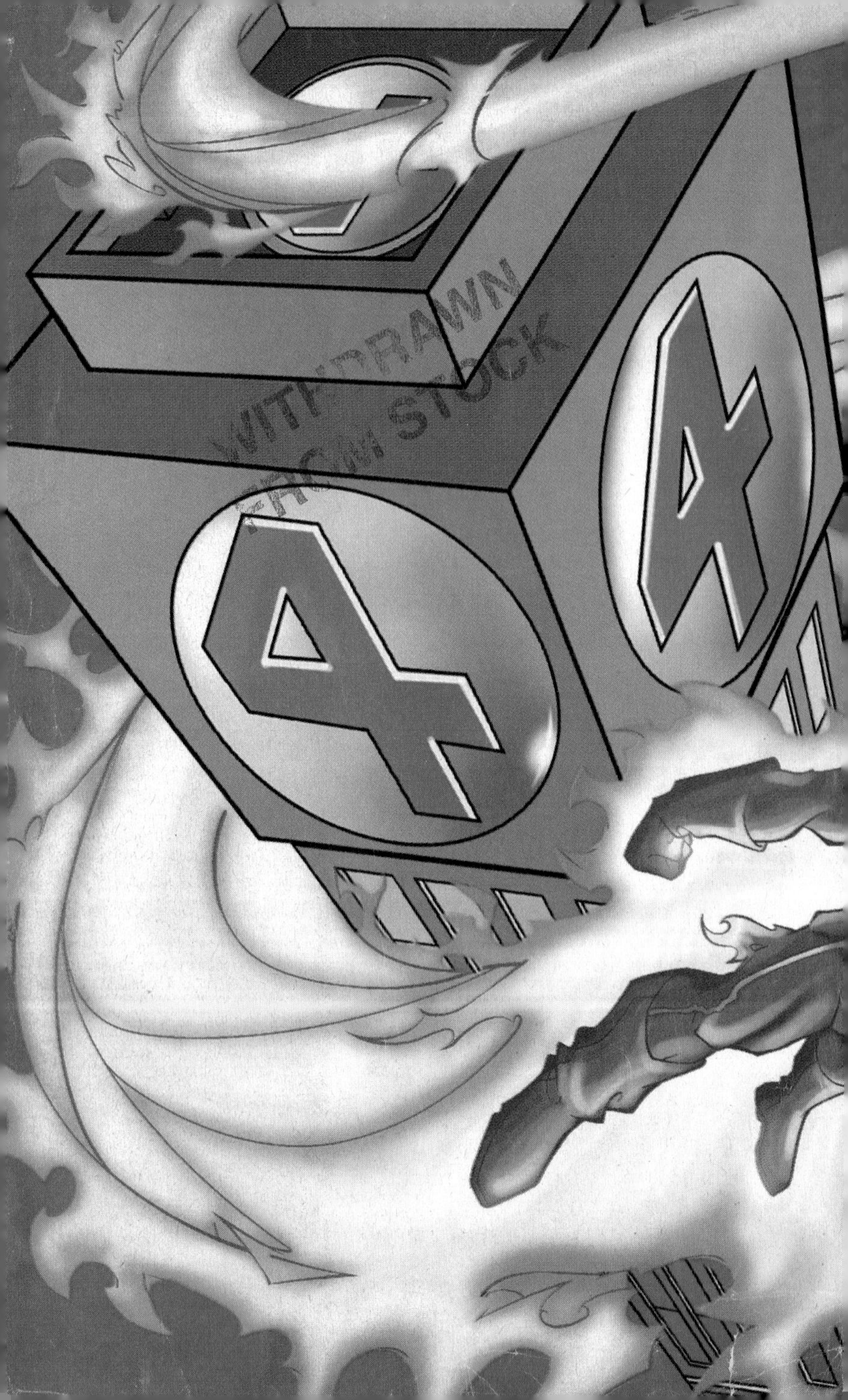

Fantastic Four DOOM

Plot: Stan Lee & Jack Kirby
Script: Marc Sumerak & John Layman
Pencilers: Alitha Martinez
& Joe Dodd
Inkers: Robert Campanella
& Justin Holman
Colorist: Gotham
Letterer: Dave Sharpe
Cover Art: Makoto Nakatsuka
& SotoColor's J. Rauch

Assistant Editors: John Barber
& MacKenzie Cadenhead
Editor: C.B. Cebulski
Consulting Edtior: Ralph Macchio
Sales Manager: David Gabriel

Collections Editor: Jeff Youngquist
Assistant Editor: Jennifer Grünwald
Book Designer: Carrie Beadle
Creative Director: Tom Marvelli

Editor in Chief: Joe Quesada
Publisher: Dan Buckley

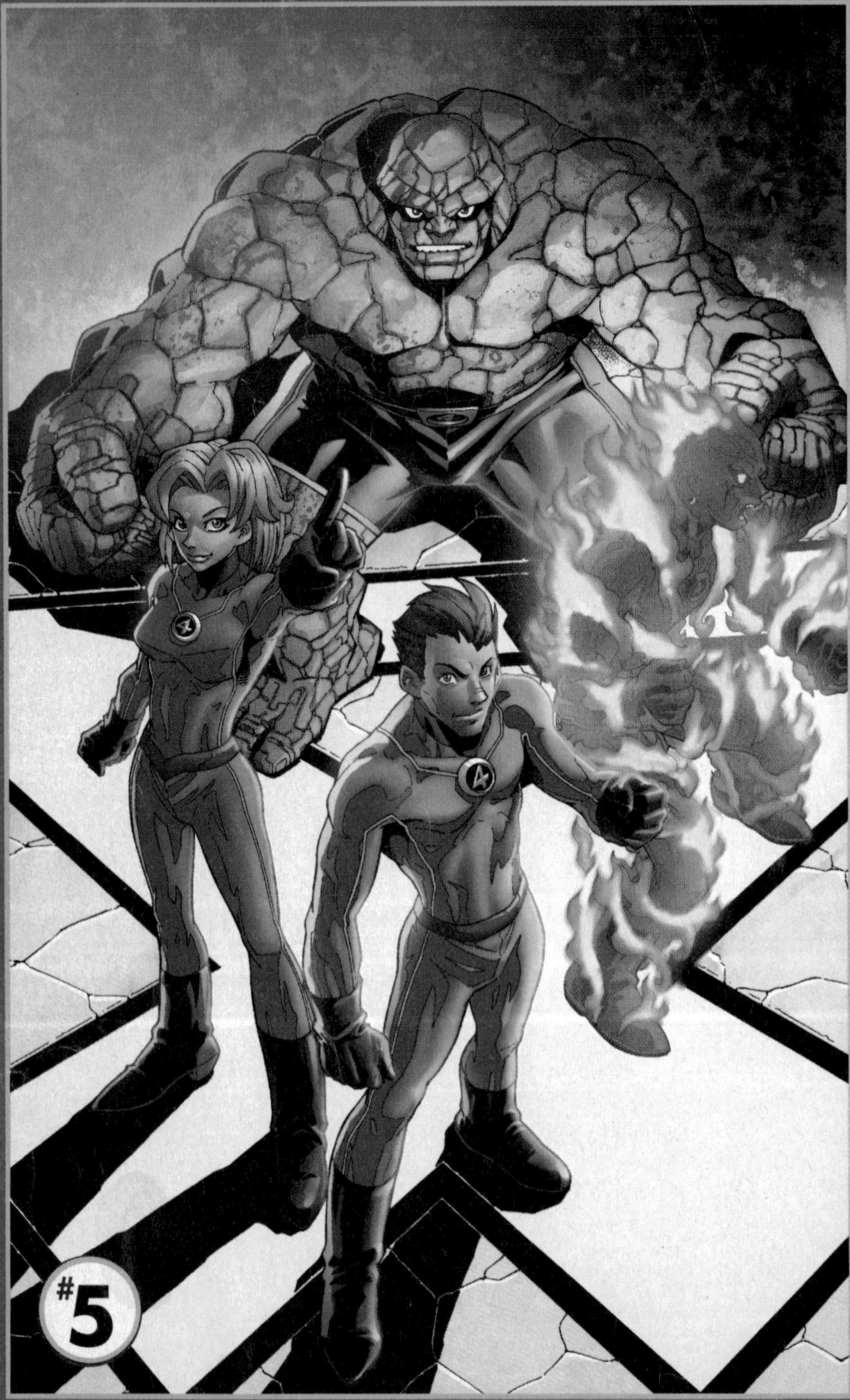
#5

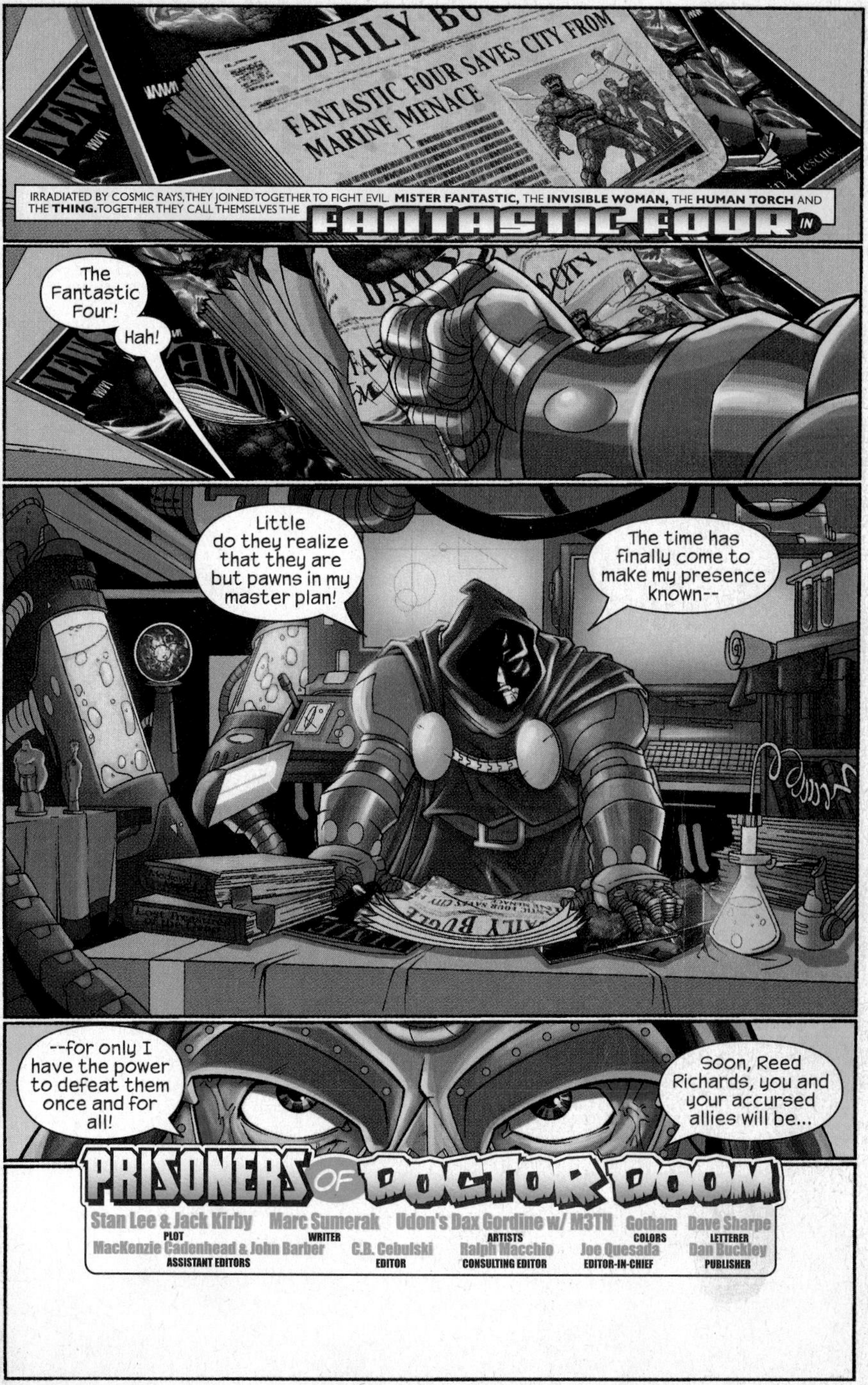
DAILY BUGLE
FANTASTIC FOUR SAVES CITY FROM MARINE MENACE
IRRADIATED BY COSMIC RAYS, THEY JOINED TOGETHER TO FIGHT EVIL. **MISTER FANTASTIC,** THE **INVISIBLE WOMAN,** THE **HUMAN TORCH** AND THE **THING.** TOGETHER THEY CALL THEMSELVES THE FANTASTIC FOUR IN
The Fantastic Four!
Hah!
Little do they realize that they are but pawns in my master plan!
The time has finally come to make my presence known--
--for only I have the power to defeat them once and for all!
Soon, Reed Richards, you and your accursed allies will be...
PRISONERS OF DOCTOR DOOM
Stan Lee & Jack Kirby PLOT
Marc Sumerak WRITER
Udon's Dax Gordine w/ M3TH ARTISTS
Gotham COLORS
Dave Sharpe LETTERER
MacKenzie Cadenhead & John Barber ASSISTANT EDITORS
C.B. Cebulski EDITOR
Ralph Macchio CONSULTING EDITOR
Joe Quesada EDITOR-IN-CHIEF
Dan Buckley PUBLISHER

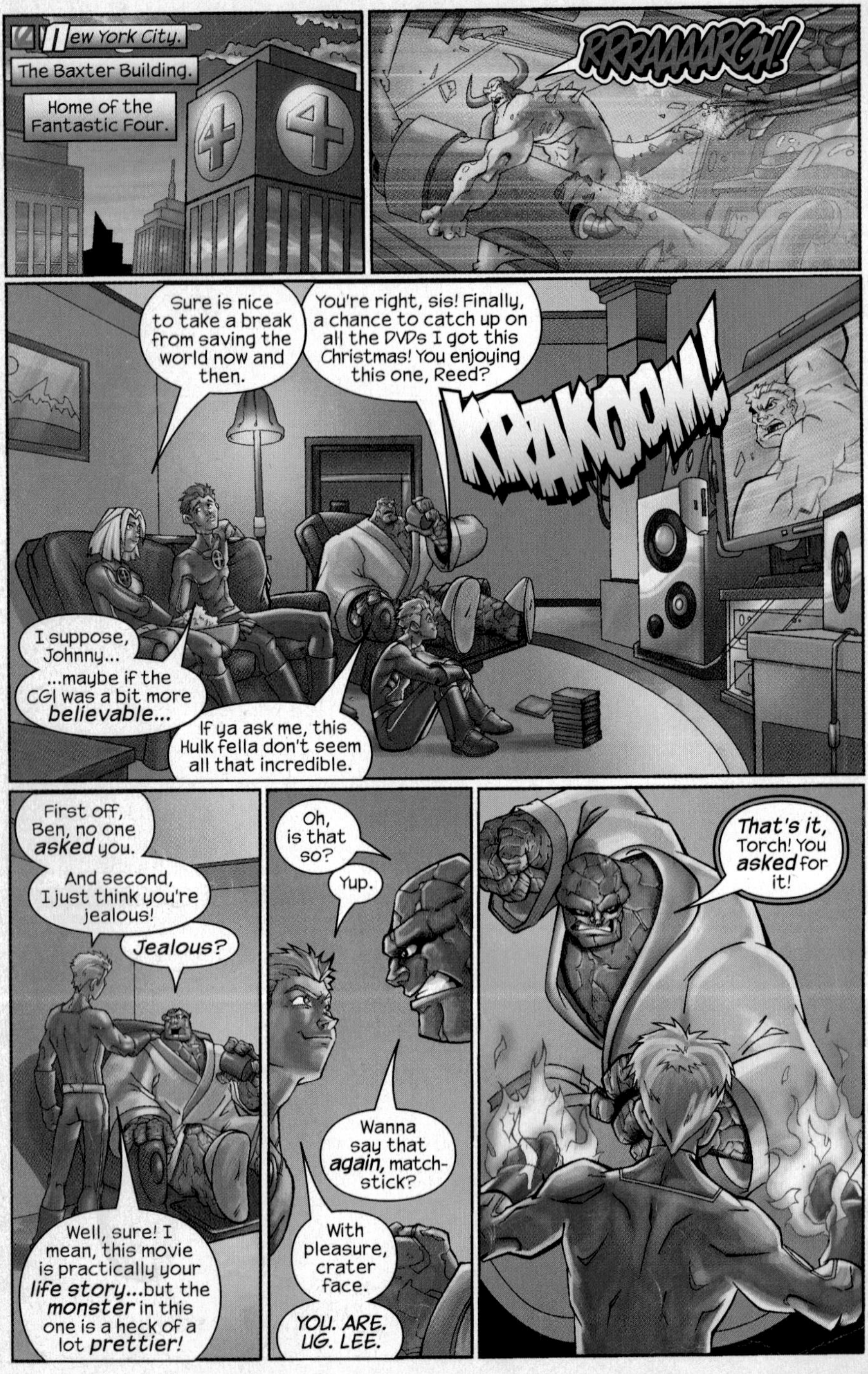
New York City.
The Baxter Building.
Home of the Fantastic Four.
RRRAAAARGH!
Sure is nice to take a break from saving the world now and then.
You're right, sis! Finally, a chance to catch up on all the DVDs I got this Christmas! You enjoying this one, Reed?
KRAKOOM!
I suppose, Johnny...
...maybe if the CGI was a bit more believable...
If ya ask me, this Hulk fella don't seem all that incredible.
First off, Ben, no one asked you.
And second, I just think you're jealous!
Jealous?
Well, sure! I mean, this movie is practically your life story...but the monster in this one is a heck of a lot prettier!
Oh, is that so?
Yup.
Wanna say that again, match-stick?
With pleasure, crater face.
YOU. ARE. UG. LEE.
That's it, Torch! You asked for it!

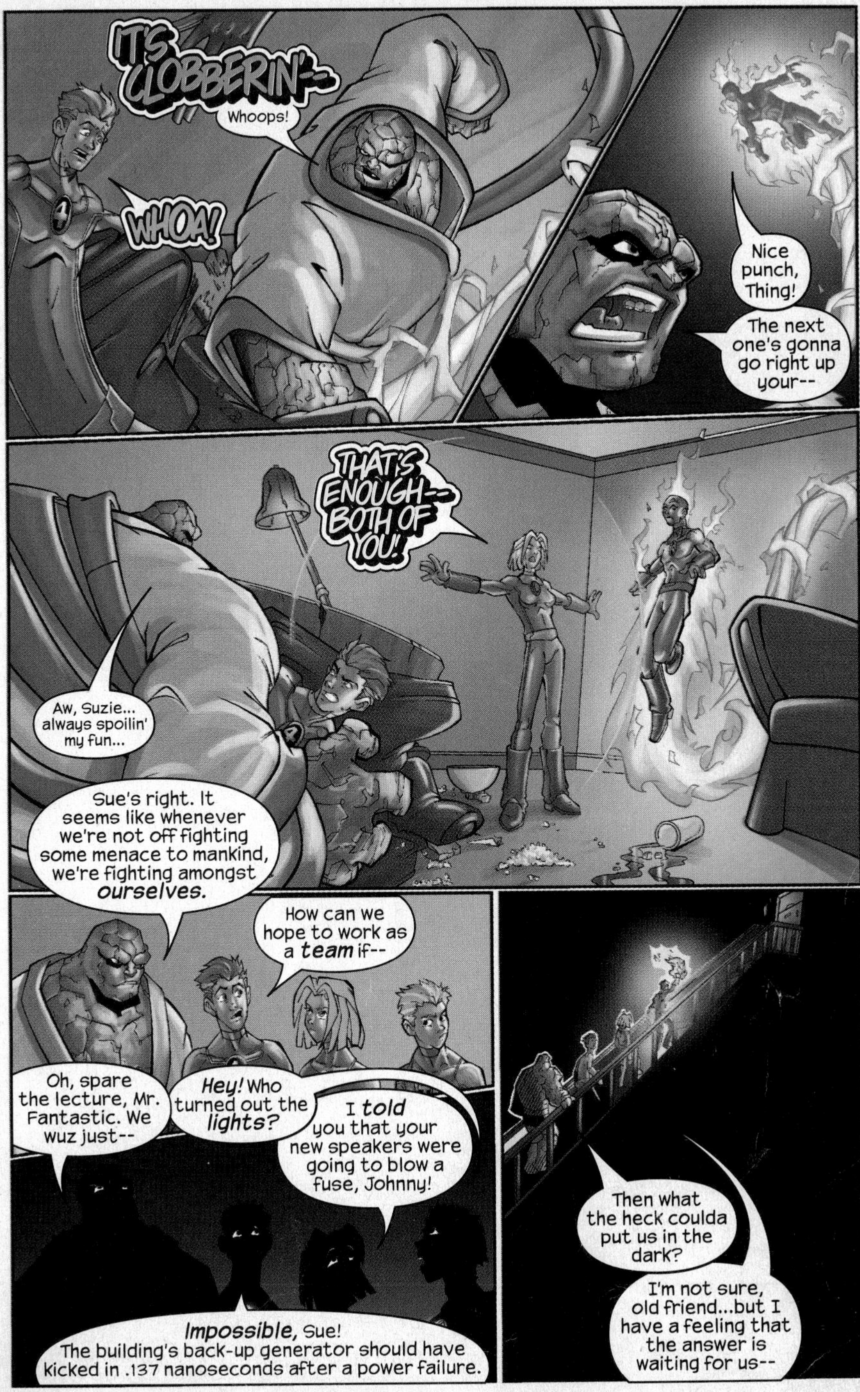
IT'S CLOBBERIN'--
Whoops!
WHOA!
Nice punch, Thing!
The next one's gonna go right up your--
THAT'S ENOUGH--BOTH OF YOU!
Aw, Suzie... always spoilin' my fun...
Sue's right. It seems like whenever we're not off fighting some menace to mankind, we're fighting amongst *ourselves.*
How can we hope to work as a *team* if--
Oh, spare the lecture, Mr. Fantastic. We wuz just--
Hey! Who turned out the *lights?*
I *told* you that your new speakers were going to blow a fuse, Johnny!
Impossible, Sue! The building's back-up generator should have kicked in .137 nanoseconds after a power failure.
Then what the heck coulda put us in the dark?
I'm not sure, old friend...but I have a feeling that the answer is waiting for us--

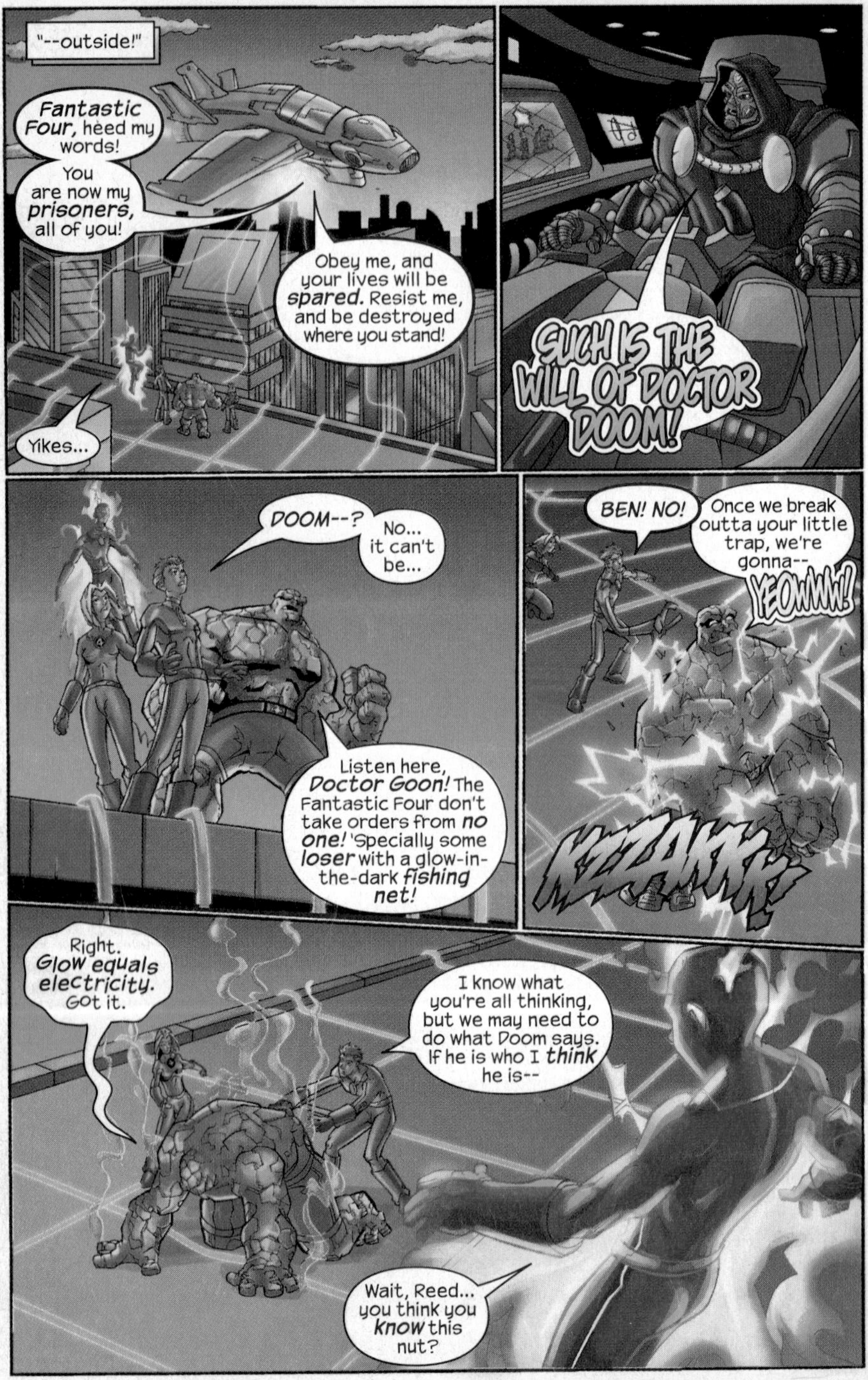
"--outside!"
Fantastic Four, heed my words!
You are now my prisoners, all of you!
Obey me, and your lives will be spared. Resist me, and be destroyed where you stand!
Yikes...
SUCH IS THE WILL OF DOCTOR DOOM!
DOOM--?
No... it can't be...
Listen here, Doctor Goon! The Fantastic Four don't take orders from no one! 'Specially some loser with a glow-in-the-dark fishing net!
BEN! NO!
Once we break outta your little trap, we're gonna--
YEOWWW!
KRZZAKKK!
Right. Glow equals electricity. Got it.
I know what you're all thinking, but we may need to do what Doom says. If he is who I think he is--
Wait, Reed... you think you know this nut?

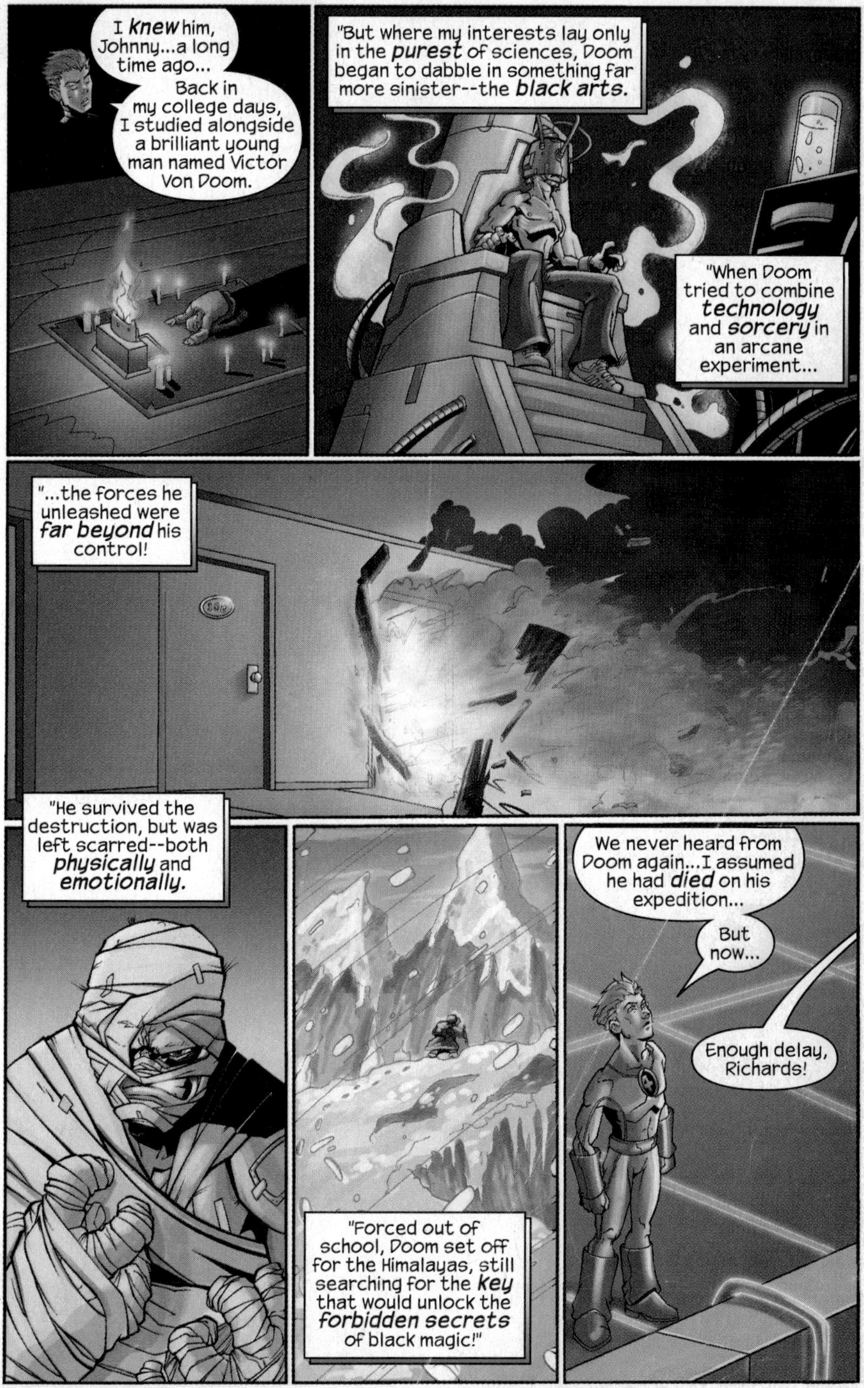
I knew him, Johnny...a long time ago...
Back in my college days, I studied alongside a brilliant young man named Victor Von Doom.
"But where my interests lay only in the purest of sciences, Doom began to dabble in something far more sinister--the black arts.
"When Doom tried to combine technology and sorcery in an arcane experiment...
"...the forces he unleashed were far beyond his control!
"He survived the destruction, but was left scarred--both physically and emotionally.
"Forced out of school, Doom set off for the Himalayas, still searching for the key that would unlock the forbidden secrets of black magic!"
We never heard from Doom again...I assumed he had died on his expedition...
But now...
Enough delay, Richards!

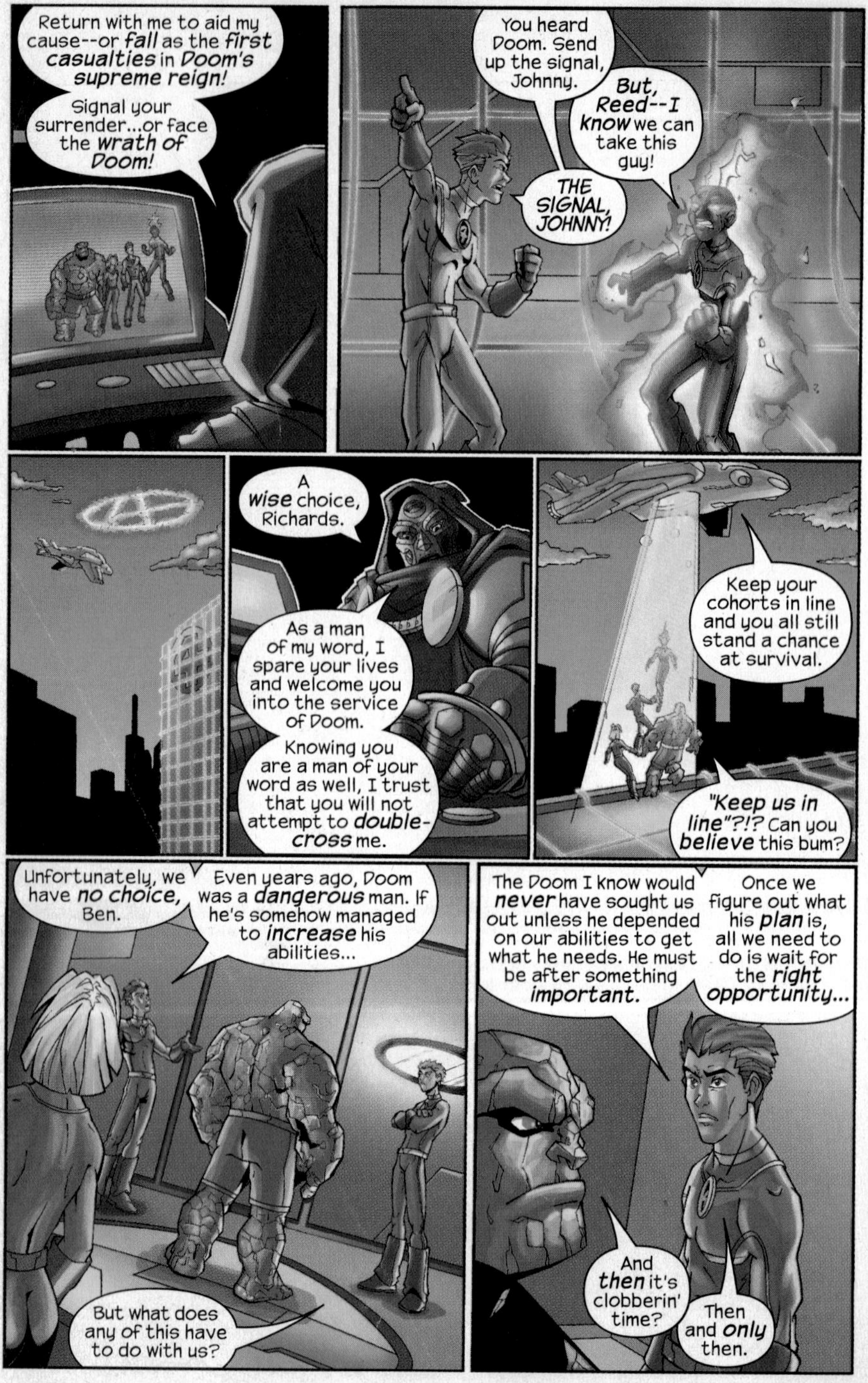
Return with me to aid my cause--or fall as the first casualties in Doom's supreme reign!
Signal your surrender...or face the wrath of Doom!
You heard Doom. Send up the signal, Johnny.
But, Reed--I know we can take this guy!
THE SIGNAL, JOHNNY!
A wise choice, Richards.
As a man of my word, I spare your lives and welcome you into the service of Doom.
Knowing you are a man of your word as well, I trust that you will not attempt to double-cross me.
Keep your cohorts in line and you all still stand a chance at survival.
"Keep us in line"?!? Can you believe this bum?
Unfortunately, we have no choice, Ben.
Even years ago, Doom was a dangerous man. If he's somehow managed to increase his abilities...
But what does any of this have to do with us?
The Doom I know would never have sought us out unless he depended on our abilities to get what he needs. He must be after something important.
Once we figure out what his plan is, all we need to do is wait for the right opportunity...
And then it's clobberin' time?
Then and only then.

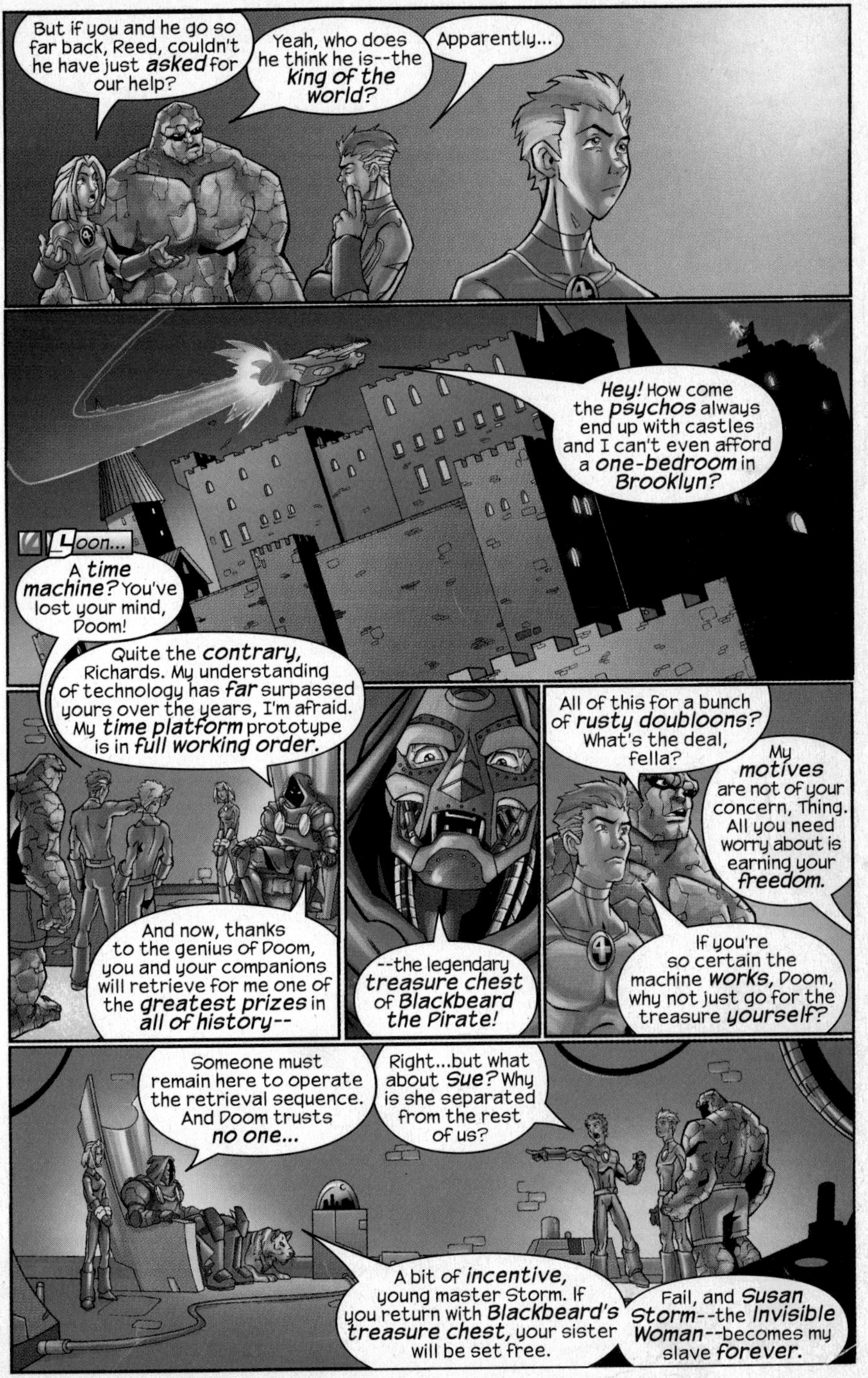
But if you and he go so far back, Reed, couldn't he have just asked for our help?
Yeah, who does he think he is--the king of the world?
Apparently...
Hey! How come the psychos always end up with castles and I can't even afford a one-bedroom in Brooklyn?
Soon...
A time machine? You've lost your mind, Doom!
Quite the contrary, Richards. My understanding of technology has far surpassed yours over the years, I'm afraid. My time platform prototype is in full working order.
And now, thanks to the genius of Doom, you and your companions will retrieve for me one of the greatest prizes in all of history--
--the legendary treasure chest of Blackbeard the Pirate!
All of this for a bunch of rusty doubloons? What's the deal, fella?
My motives are not of your concern, Thing. All you need worry about is earning your freedom.
If you're so certain the machine works, Doom, why not just go for the treasure yourself?
Someone must remain here to operate the retrieval sequence. And Doom trusts no one...
Right...but what about Sue? Why is she separated from the rest of us?
A bit of incentive, young master Storm. If you return with Blackbeard's treasure chest, your sister will be set free.
Fail, and Susan Storm--the Invisible Woman--becomes my slave forever.

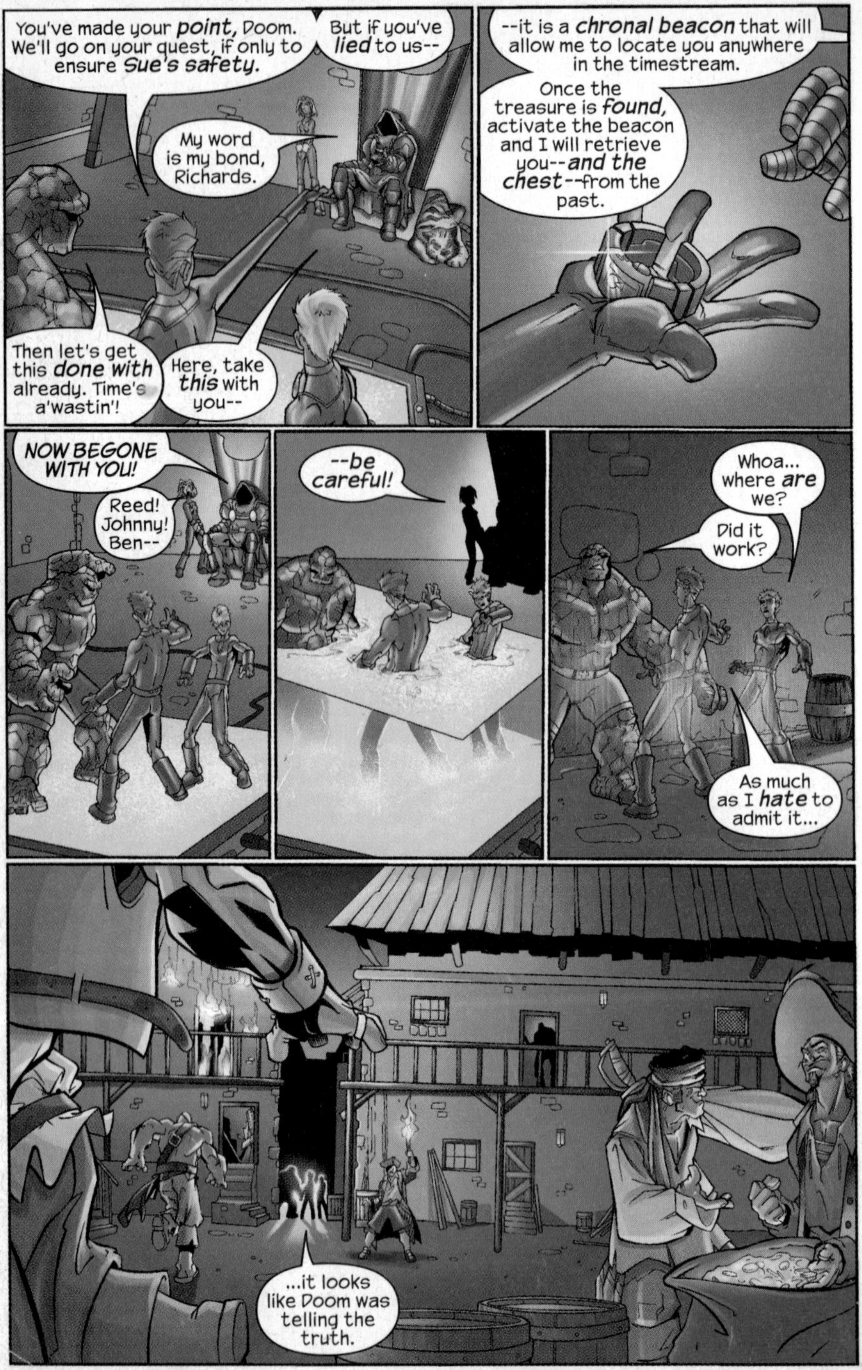
You've made your point, Doom. We'll go on your quest, if only to ensure Sue's safety.
But if you've lied to us--
My word is my bond, Richards.
Then let's get this done with already. Time's a'wastin'!
Here, take this with you--
--it is a chronal beacon that will allow me to locate you anywhere in the timestream.
Once the treasure is found, activate the beacon and I will retrieve you--and the chest--from the past.
NOW BEGONE WITH YOU!
Reed! Johnny! Ben--
--be careful!
Whoa... where are we?
Did it work?
As much as I hate to admit it...
...it looks like Doom was telling the truth.

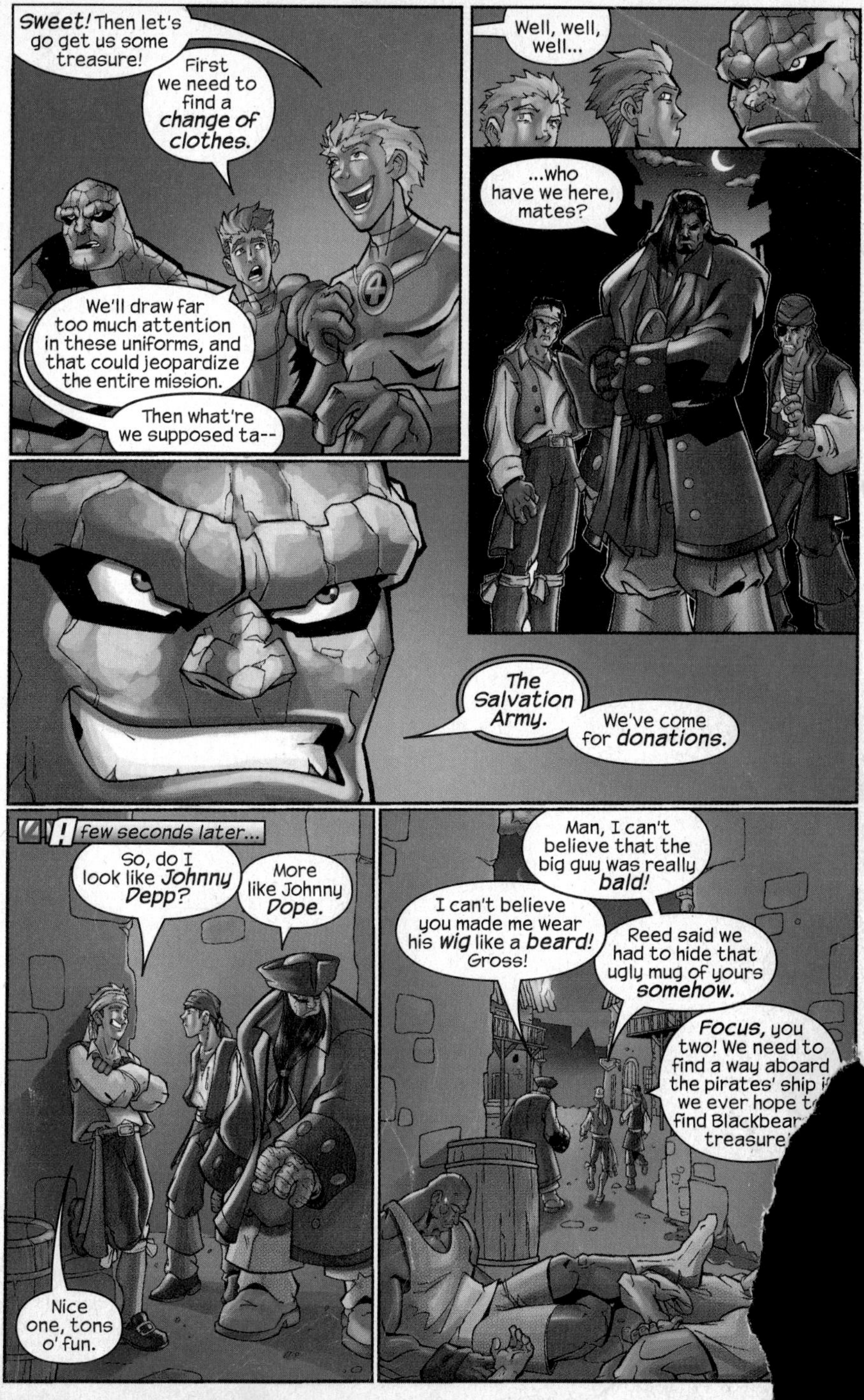
Sweet! Then let's go get us some treasure!
First we need to find a change of clothes.
We'll draw far too much attention in these uniforms, and that could jeopardize the entire mission.
Then what're we supposed ta--
Well, well, well...
...who have we here, mates?
The Salvation Army.
We've come for donations.
A few seconds later...
So, do I look like Johnny Depp?
More like Johnny Dope.
Nice one, tons o' fun.
Man, I can't believe that the big guy was really bald!
I can't believe you made me wear his wig like a beard! Gross!
Reed said we had to hide that ugly mug of yours somehow.
Focus, you two! We need to find a way aboard the pirates' ship if we ever hope t find Blackbear treasure!

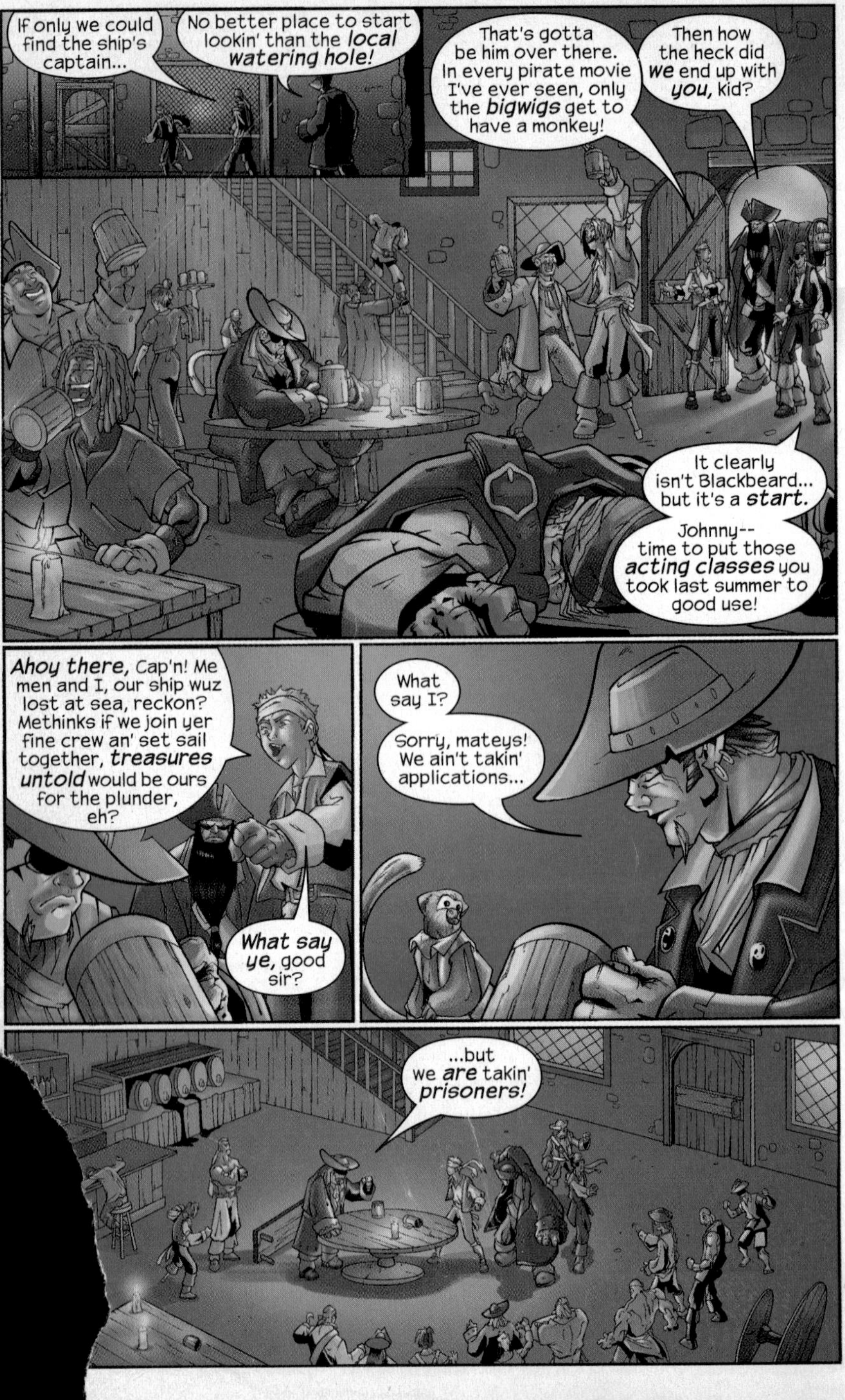

If only we could find the ship's captain...
No better place to start lookin' than the local watering hole!
That's gotta be him over there. In every pirate movie I've ever seen, only the bigwigs get to have a monkey!
Then how the heck did we end up with you, kid?
It clearly isn't Blackbeard... but it's a start.
Johnny-- time to put those acting classes you took last summer to good use!
Ahoy there, Cap'n! Me men and I, our ship wuz lost at sea, reckon? Methinks if we join yer fine crew an' set sail together, treasures untold would be ours for the plunder, eh?
What say ye, good sir?
What say I?
Sorry, mateys! We ain't takin' applications...
...but we are takin' prisoners!

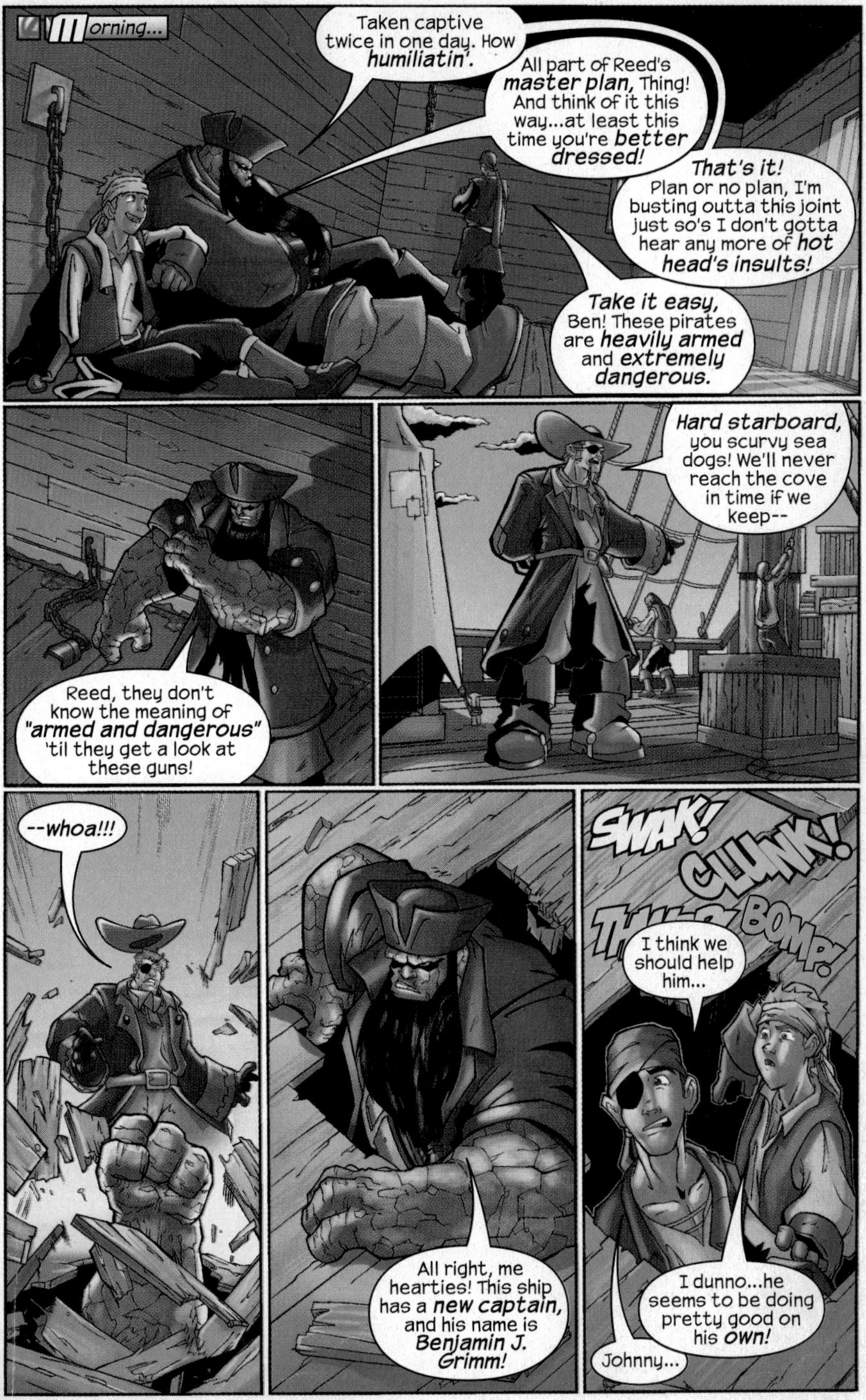
Morning...
Taken captive twice in one day. How humiliatin'.
All part of Reed's master plan, Thing! And think of it this way...at least this time you're better dressed!
That's it! Plan or no plan, I'm busting outta this joint just so's I don't gotta hear any more of hot head's insults!
Take it easy, Ben! These pirates are heavily armed and extremely dangerous.
Reed, they don't know the meaning of "armed and dangerous" 'til they get a look at these guns!
Hard starboard, you scurvy sea dogs! We'll never reach the cove in time if we keep--
--whoa!!!
All right, me hearties! This ship has a new captain, and his name is Benjamin J. Grimm!
SWAK!
CLUNK!
BOMP!
I think we should help him...
I dunno...he seems to be doing pretty good on his own!
Johnny...

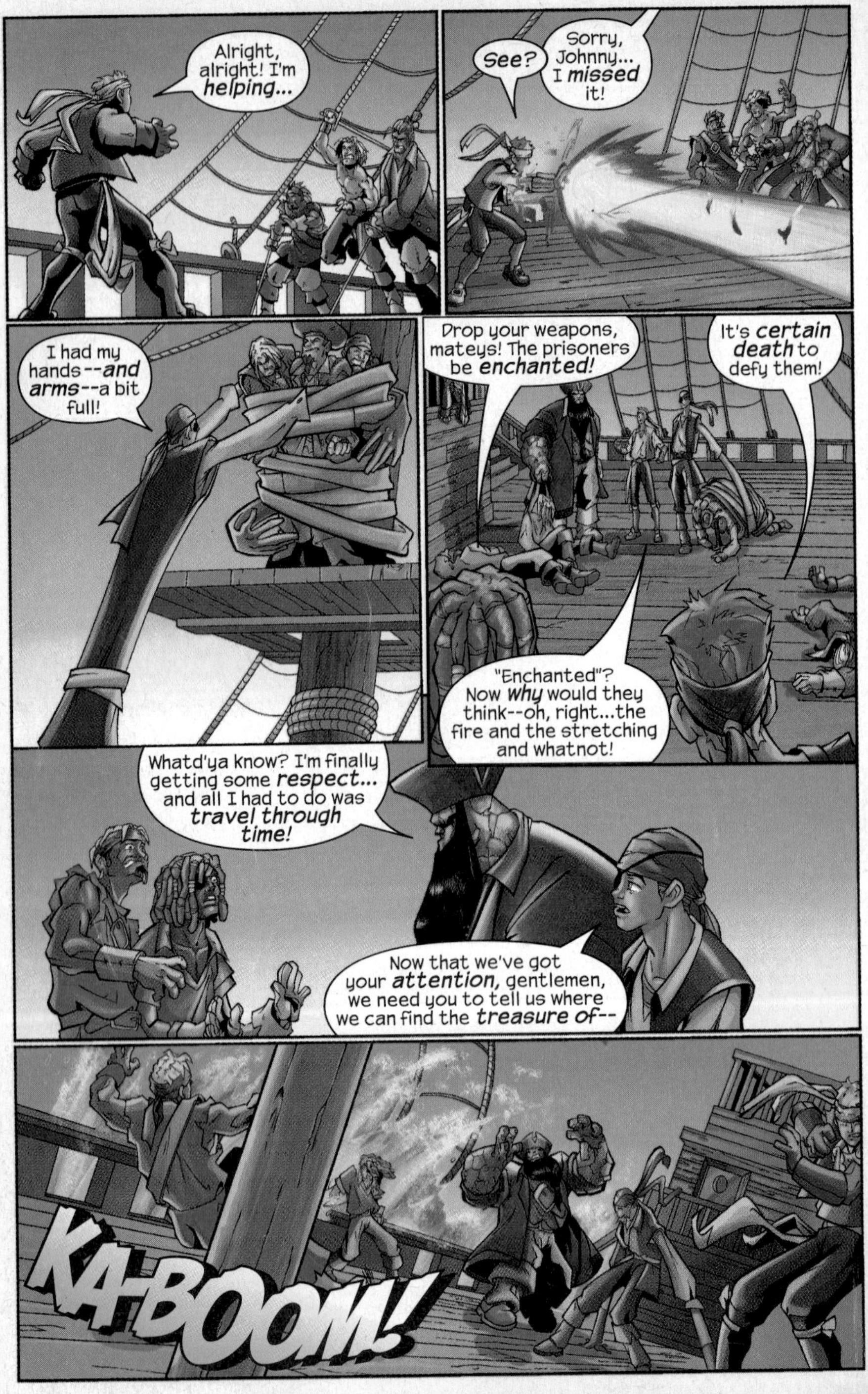
Alright, alright! I'm helping...
See?
Sorry, Johnny... I missed it!
I had my hands--and arms--a bit full!
Drop your weapons, mateys! The prisoners be enchanted!
It's certain death to defy them!
"Enchanted"? Now why would they think--oh, right...the fire and the stretching and whatnot!
Whatd'ya know? I'm finally getting some respect... and all I had to do was travel through time!
Now that we've got your attention, gentlemen, we need you to tell us where we can find the treasure of--
KA-BOOM!

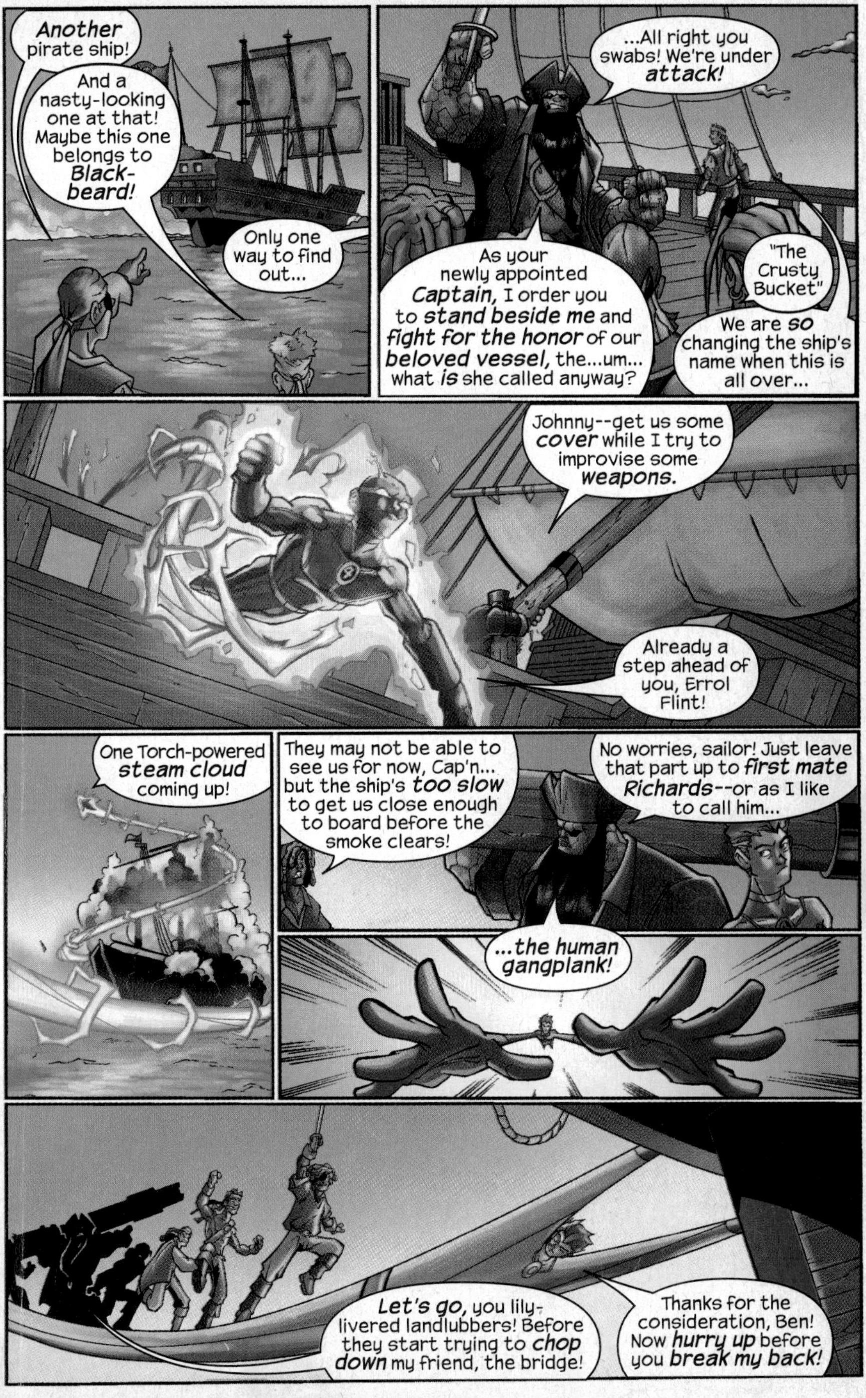

Another pirate ship!
And a nasty-looking one at that! Maybe this one belongs to Black-beard!
Only one way to find out...
...All right you swabs! We're under attack!
As your newly appointed Captain, I order you to stand beside me and fight for the honor of our beloved vessel, the...um... what is she called anyway?
"The Crusty Bucket"
We are so changing the ship's name when this is all over...
Johnny--get us some cover while I try to improvise some weapons.
Already a step ahead of you, Errol Flint!
One Torch-powered steam cloud coming up!
They may not be able to see us for now, Cap'n... but the ship's too slow to get us close enough to board before the smoke clears!
No worries, sailor! Just leave that part up to first mate Richards--or as I like to call him...
...the human gangplank!
Let's go, you lily-livered landlubbers! Before they start trying to chop down my friend, the bridge!
Thanks for the consideration, Ben! Now hurry up before you break my back!

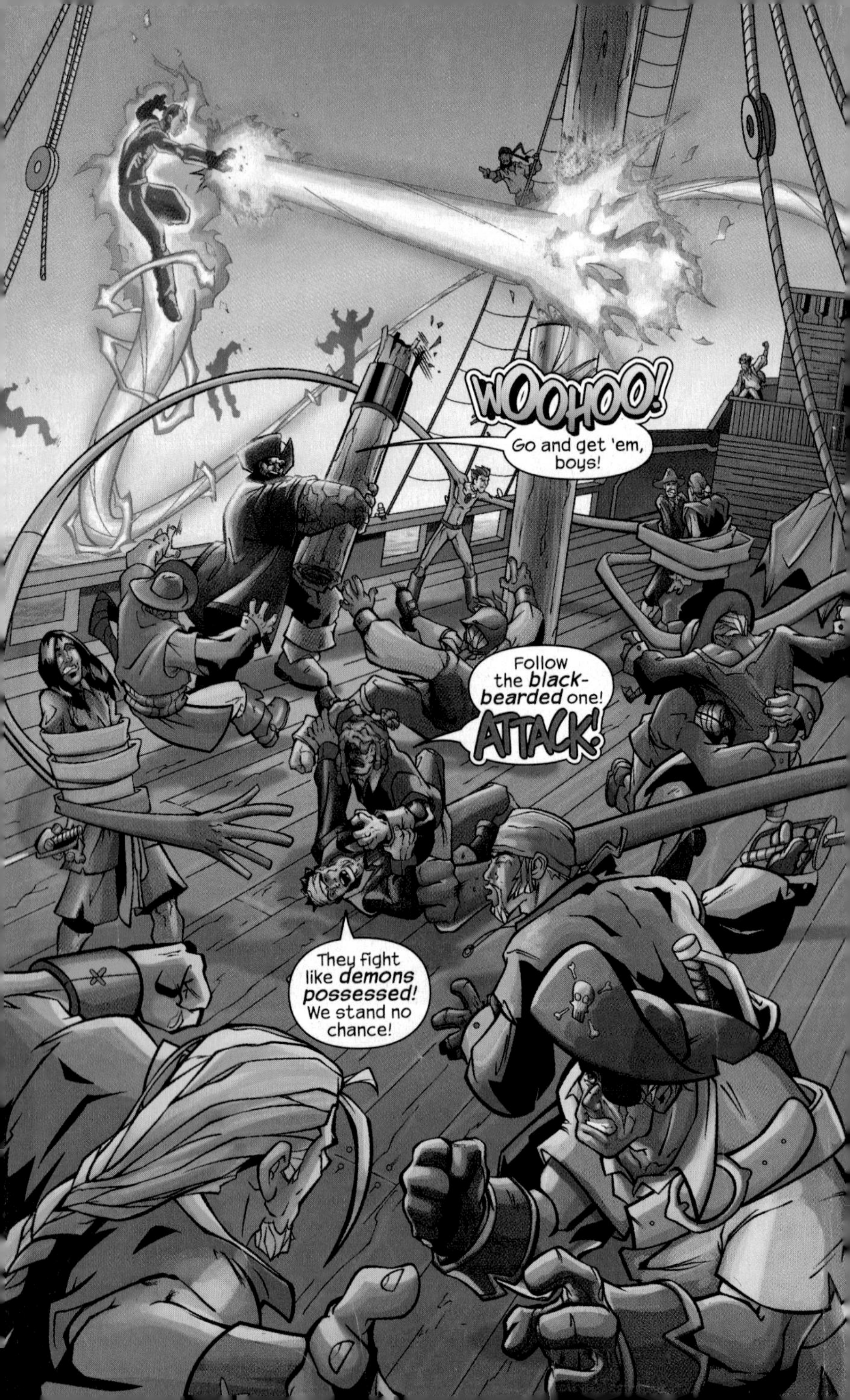
WOOHOO!
Go and get 'em, boys!
Follow the black-bearded one! ATTACK!
They fight like demons possessed! We stand no chance!

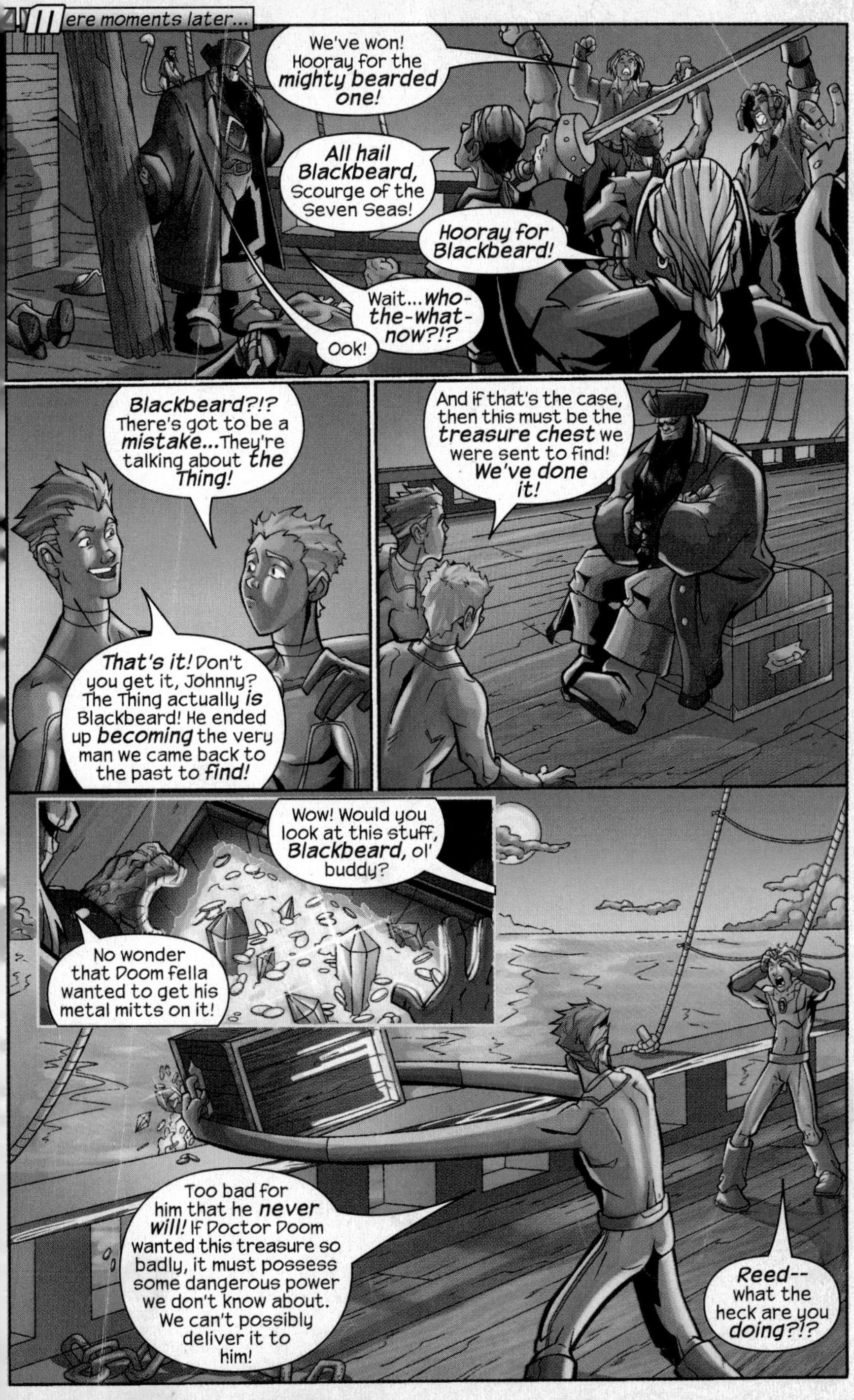
Mere moments later...
We've won! Hooray for the mighty bearded one!
All hail Blackbeard, Scourge of the Seven Seas!
Hooray for Blackbeard!
Wait...who-the-what-now?!?
Ook!
Blackbeard?!? There's got to be a mistake...They're talking about the Thing!
That's it! Don't you get it, Johnny? The Thing actually is Blackbeard! He ended up becoming the very man we came back to the past to find!
And if that's the case, then this must be the treasure chest we were sent to find! We've done it!
Wow! Would you look at this stuff, Blackbeard, ol' buddy?
No wonder that Doom fella wanted to get his metal mitts on it!
Too bad for him that he never will! If Doctor Doom wanted this treasure so badly, it must possess some dangerous power we don't know about. We can't possibly deliver it to him!
Reed-- what the heck are you doing?!?

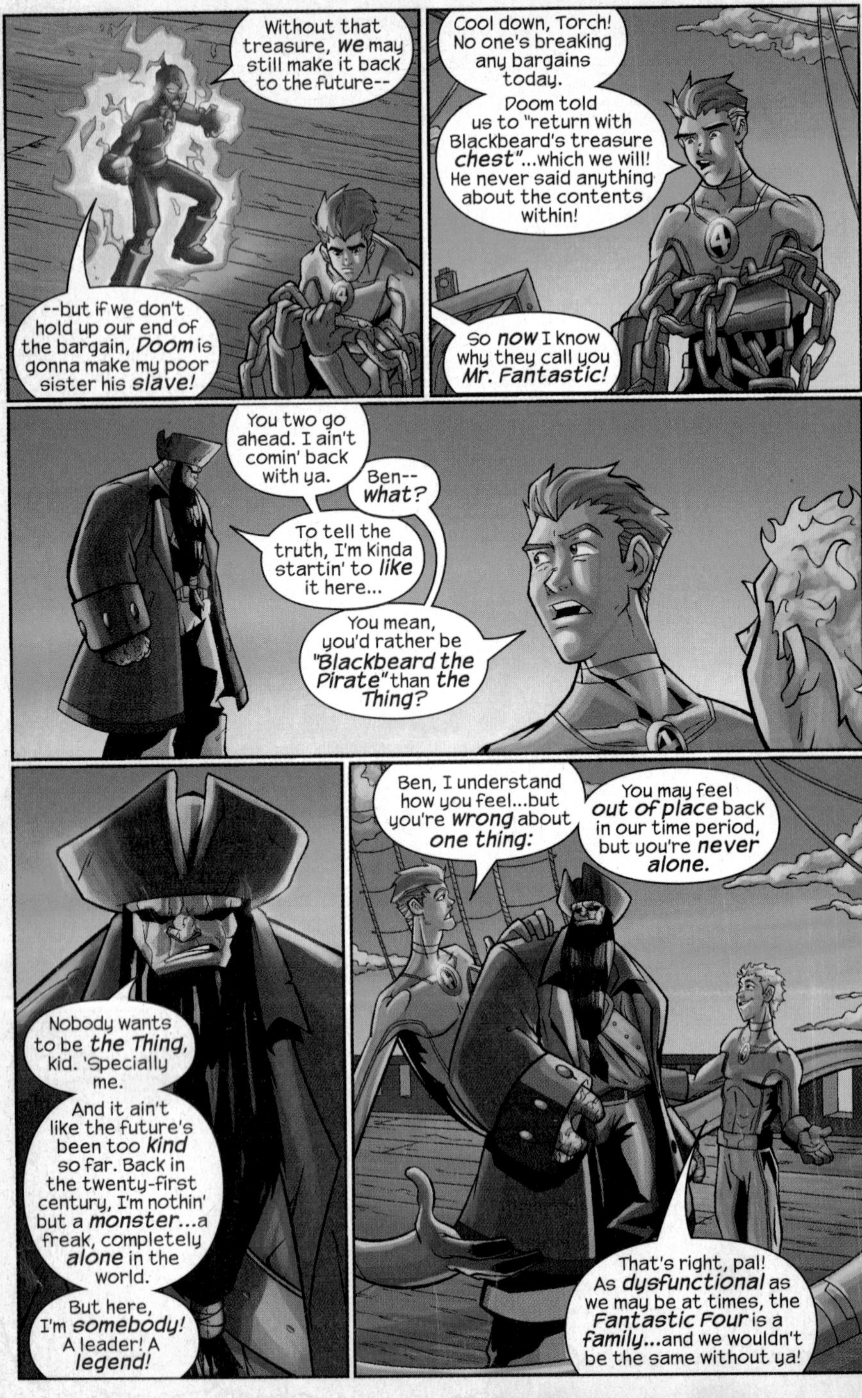
Without that treasure, *we* may still make it back to the future--
--but if we don't hold up our end of the bargain, *Doom* is gonna make my poor sister his *slave!*
Cool down, Torch! No one's breaking any bargains today.
Doom told us to "return with Blackbeard's treasure *chest*"...which we will! He never said anything about the contents within!
So *now* I know why they call you *Mr. Fantastic!*
You two go ahead. I ain't comin' back with ya.
Ben-- *what?*
To tell the truth, I'm kinda startin' to *like* it here...
You mean, you'd rather be *"Blackbeard the Pirate"* than *the Thing?*
Nobody wants to be *the Thing,* kid. 'Specially me.
And it ain't like the future's been too *kind* so far. Back in the twenty-first century, I'm nothin' but a *monster*...a freak, completely *alone* in the world.
But here, I'm *somebody!* A leader! A *legend!*
Ben, I understand how you feel...but you're *wrong* about *one thing:*
You may feel *out of place* back in our time period, but you're *never alone.*
That's right, pal! As *dysfunctional* as we may be at times, the *Fantastic Four* is a *family*...and we wouldn't be the same without ya!

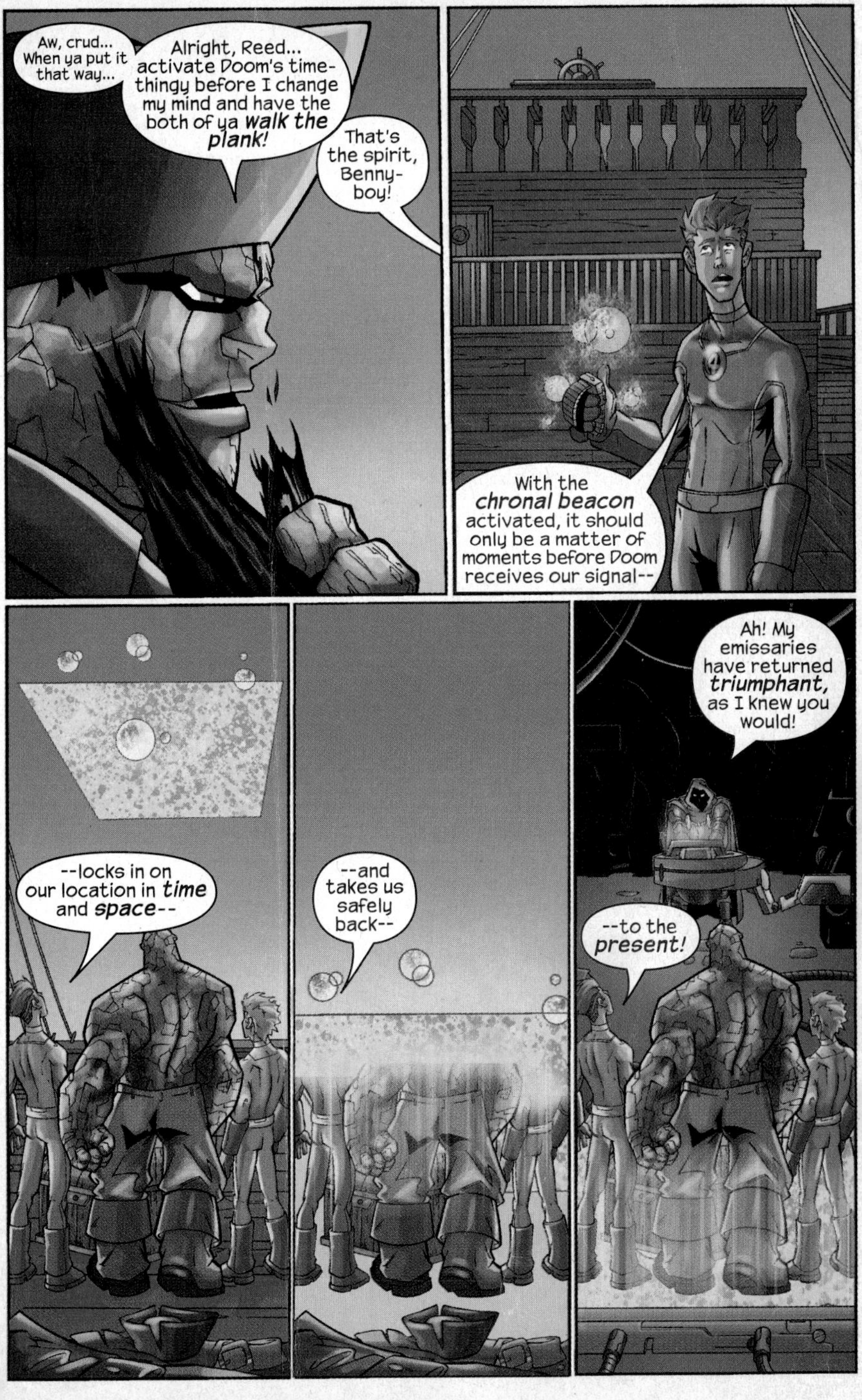
Aw, crud... When ya put it that way...
Alright, Reed... activate Doom's time-thingy before I change my mind and have the both of ya walk the plank!
That's the spirit, Benny-boy!
With the chronal beacon activated, it should only be a matter of moments before Doom receives our signal--
--locks in on our location in time and space--
--and takes us safely back--
Ah! My emissaries have returned triumphant, as I knew you would!
--to the present!

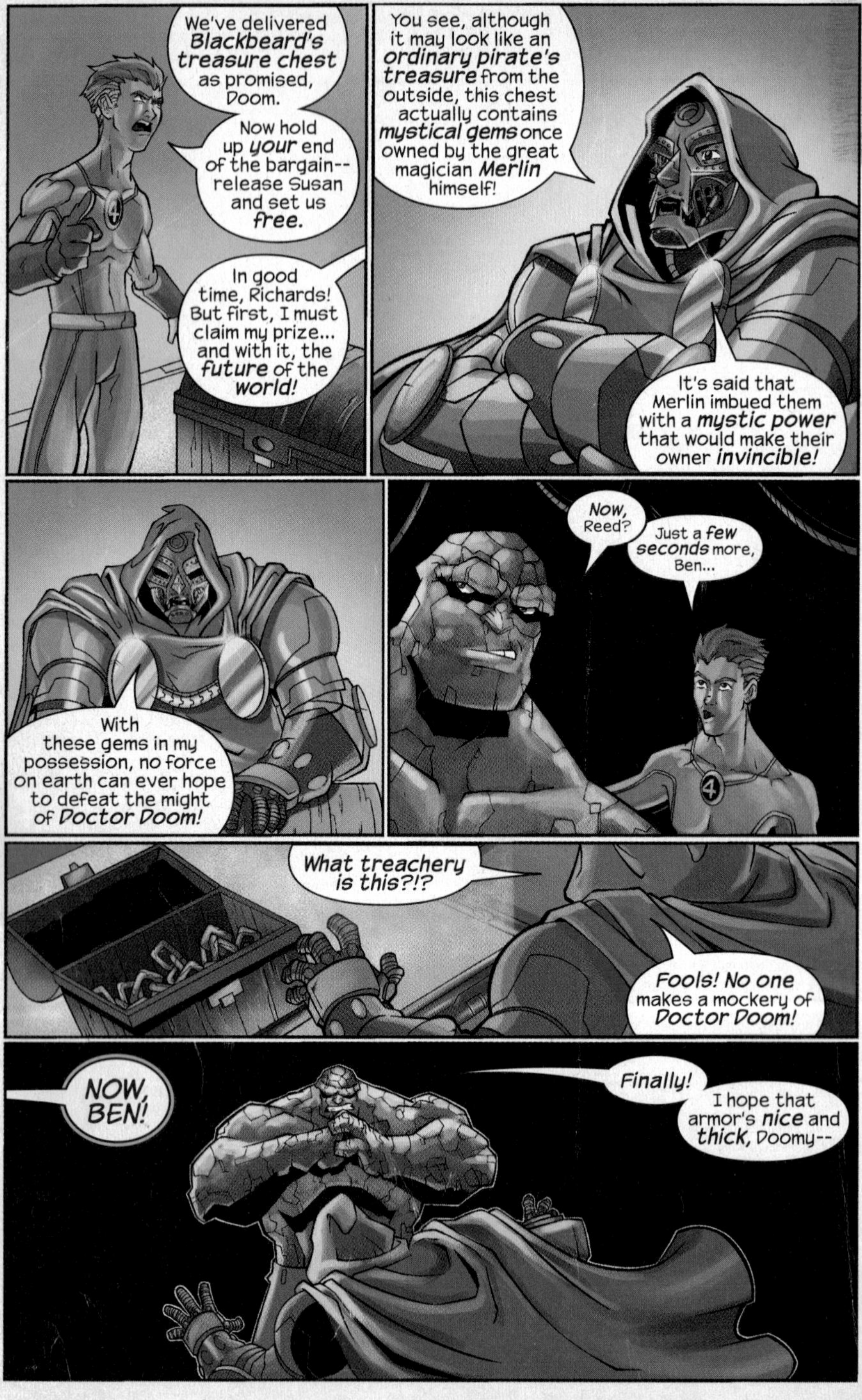
We've delivered Blackbeard's treasure chest as promised, Doom.
Now hold up your end of the bargain--release Susan and set us free.
In good time, Richards! But first, I must claim my prize... and with it, the future of the world!
You see, although it may look like an ordinary pirate's treasure from the outside, this chest actually contains mystical gems once owned by the great magician Merlin himself!
It's said that Merlin imbued them with a mystic power that would make their owner invincible!
With these gems in my possession, no force on earth can ever hope to defeat the might of Doctor Doom!
Now, Reed?
Just a few seconds more, Ben...
What treachery is this?!?
Fools! No one makes a mockery of Doctor Doom!
NOW, BEN!
Finally!
I hope that armor's nice and thick, Doomy--

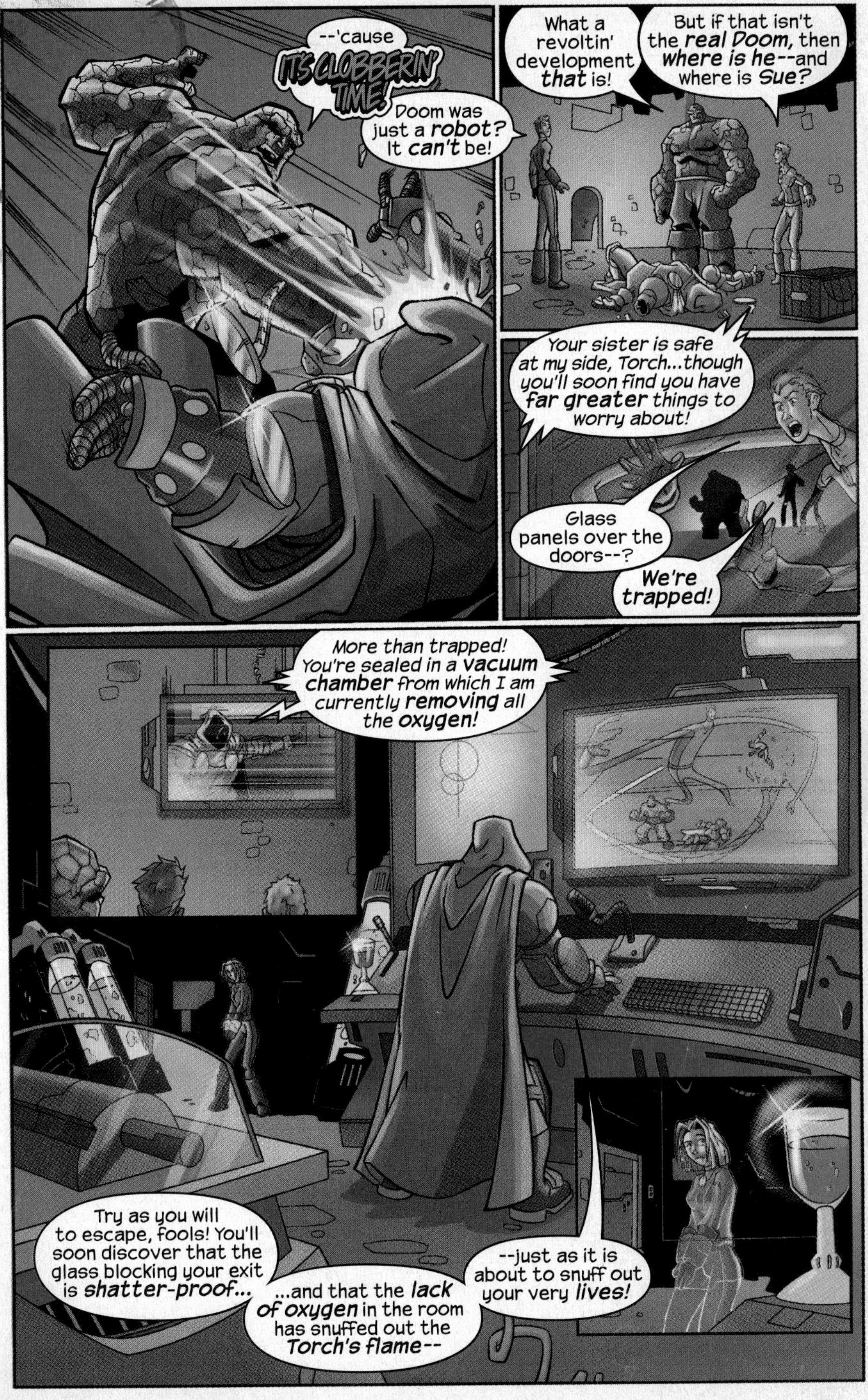

--'cause
IT'S CLOBBERIN' TIME!
Doom was just a *robot*? It *can't* be!
What a revoltin' development *that* is!
But if that isn't the *real Doom,* then *where is he*--and where is *Sue?*
Your sister is safe at my side, Torch...though you'll soon find you have *far greater* things to worry about!
Glass panels over the doors--?
We're trapped!
More than trapped! You're sealed in a *vacuum chamber* from which I am currently *removing* all the *oxygen!*
Try as you will to escape, fools! You'll soon discover that the glass blocking your exit is *shatter-proof*...
...and that the *lack of oxygen* in the room has snuffed out the *Torch's flame*--
--just as it is about to snuff out your very *lives!*

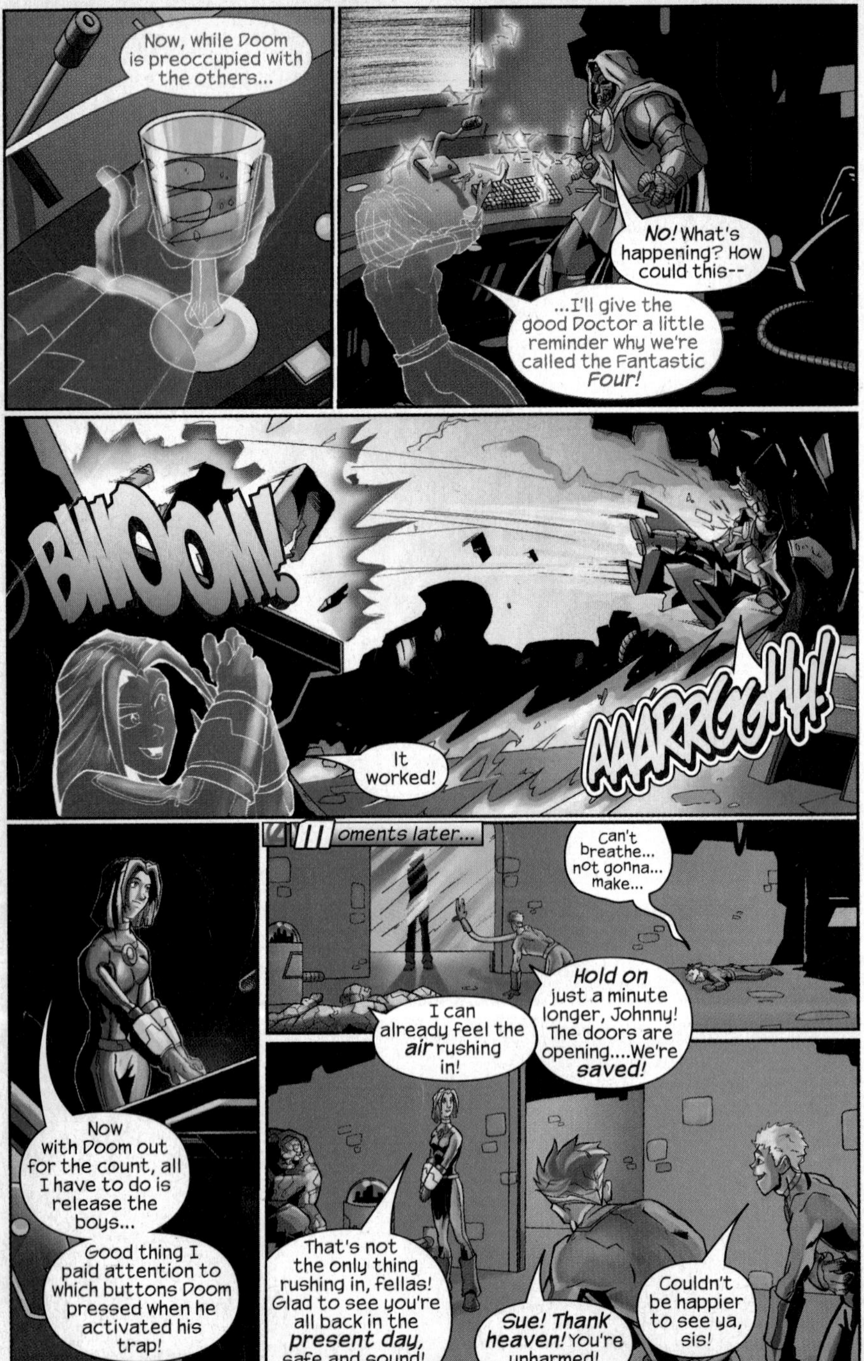

Now, while Doom is preoccupied with the others...
No! What's happening? How could this--
...I'll give the good Doctor a little reminder why we're called the Fantastic Four!
BWOOM!
It worked!
AAARRGGHH!
Now with Doom out for the count, all I have to do is release the boys...
Good thing I paid attention to which buttons Doom pressed when he activated his trap!
Moments later...
Can't breathe... not gonna... make...
Hold on just a minute longer, Johnny! The doors are opening....We're saved!
I can already feel the air rushing in!
That's not the only thing rushing in, fellas! Glad to see you're all back in the present day, safe and sound!
Sue! Thank heaven! You're unharmed!
Couldn't be happier to see ya, sis!

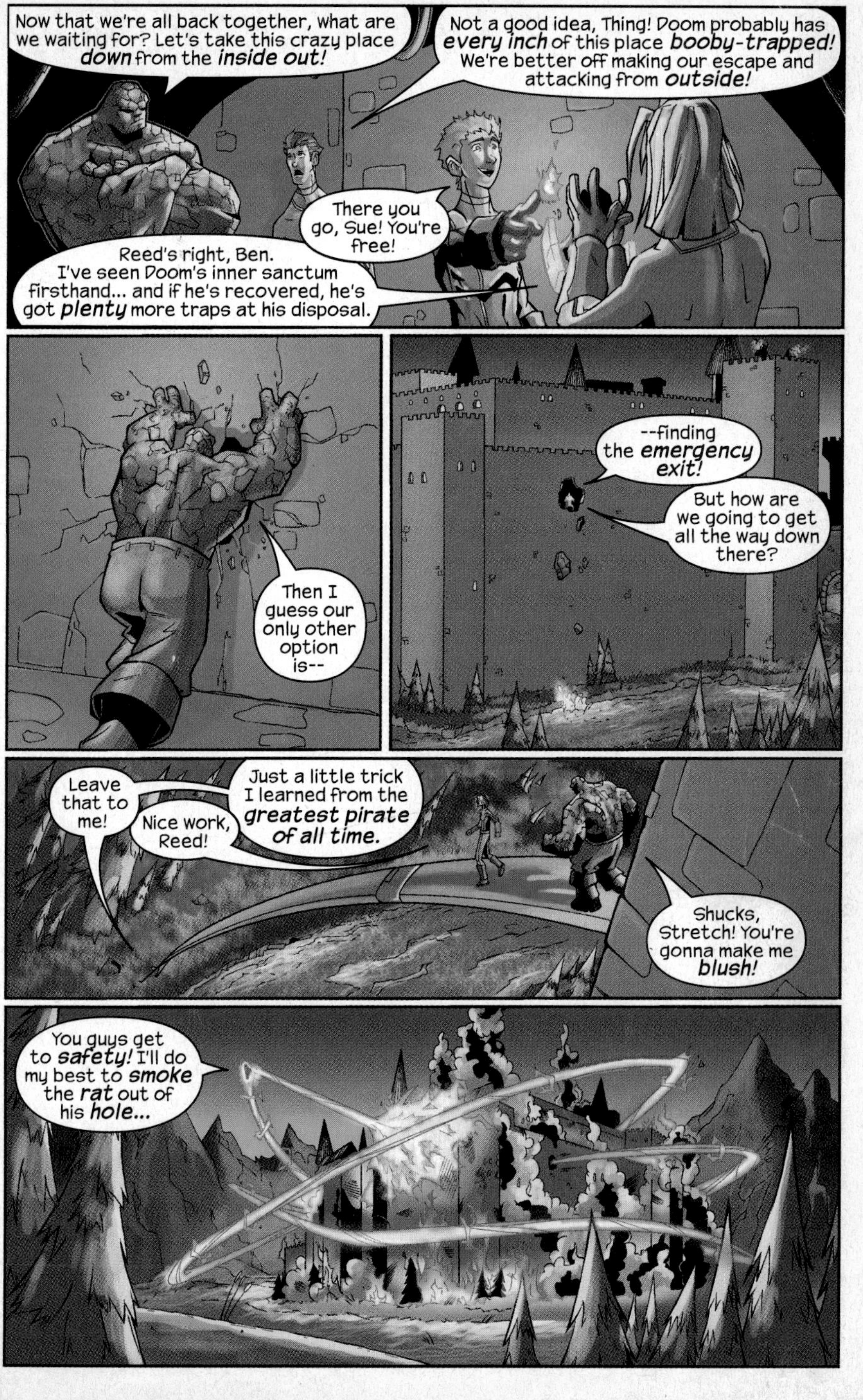
Now that we're all back together, what are we waiting for? Let's take this crazy place *down* from the *inside out!*
Not a good idea, Thing! Doom probably has *every inch* of this place *booby-trapped!* We're better off making our escape and attacking from *outside!*
There you go, Sue! You're free!
Reed's right, Ben. I've seen Doom's inner sanctum firsthand... and if he's recovered, he's got *plenty* more traps at his disposal.
Then I guess our only other option is--
--finding the *emergency exit!*
But how are we going to get all the way down there?
Leave that to me!
Nice work, Reed!
Just a little trick I learned from the *greatest pirate of all time.*
Shucks, Stretch! You're gonna make me *blush!*
You guys get to *safety!* I'll do my best to *smoke* the *rat* out of his *hole...*

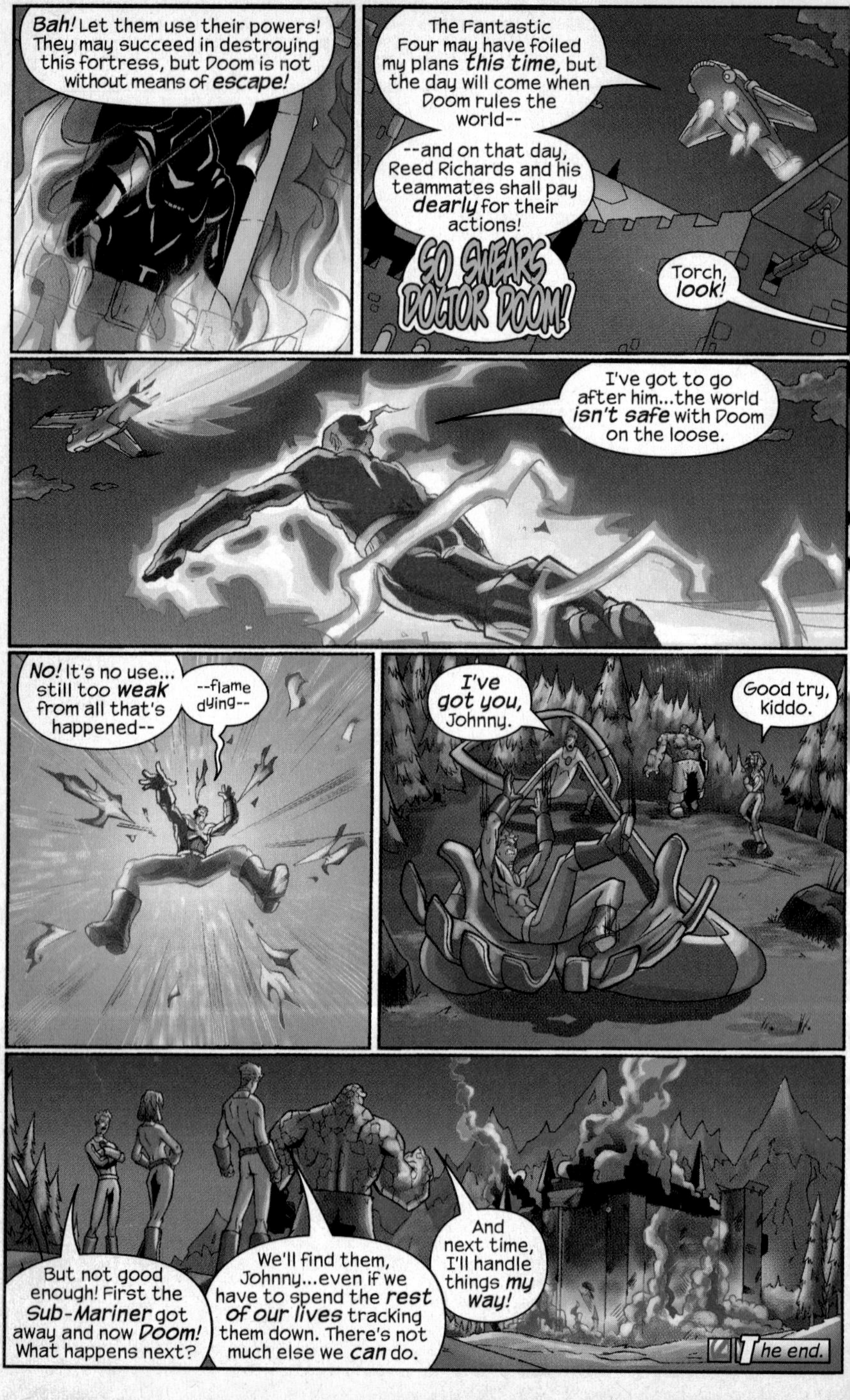

Bah! Let them use their powers! They may succeed in destroying this fortress, but Doom is not without means of escape!
The Fantastic Four may have foiled my plans this time, but the day will come when Doom rules the world--
--and on that day, Reed Richards and his teammates shall pay dearly for their actions!
SO SWEARS DOCTOR DOOM!
Torch, look!
I've got to go after him...the world isn't safe with Doom on the loose.
No! It's no use... still too weak from all that's happened--
--flame dying--
I've got you, Johnny.
Good try, kiddo.
But not good enough! First the Sub-Mariner got away and now Doom! What happens next?
We'll find them, Johnny...even if we have to spend the rest of our lives tracking them down. There's not much else we can do.
And next time, I'll handle things my way!
The end.

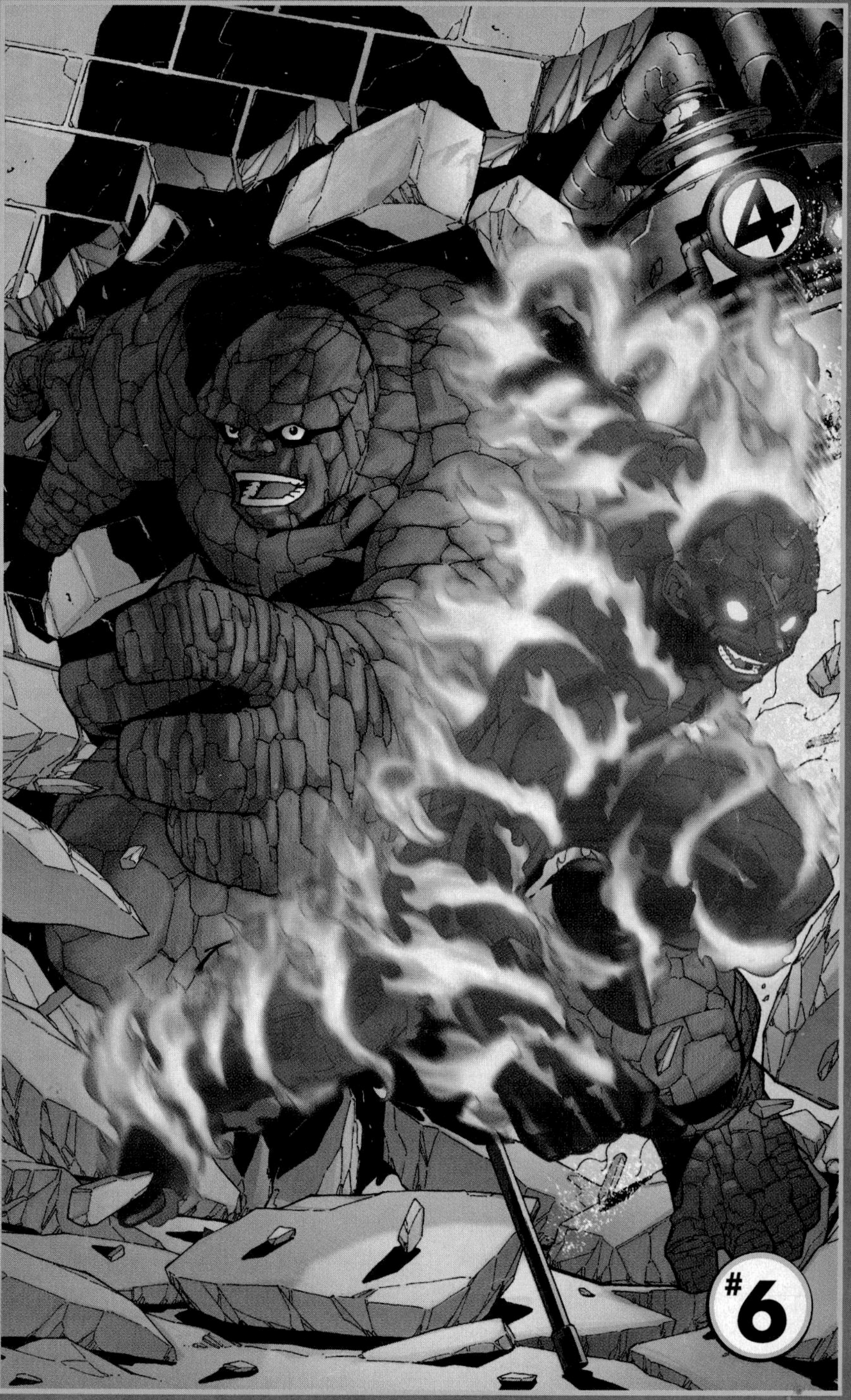
#6

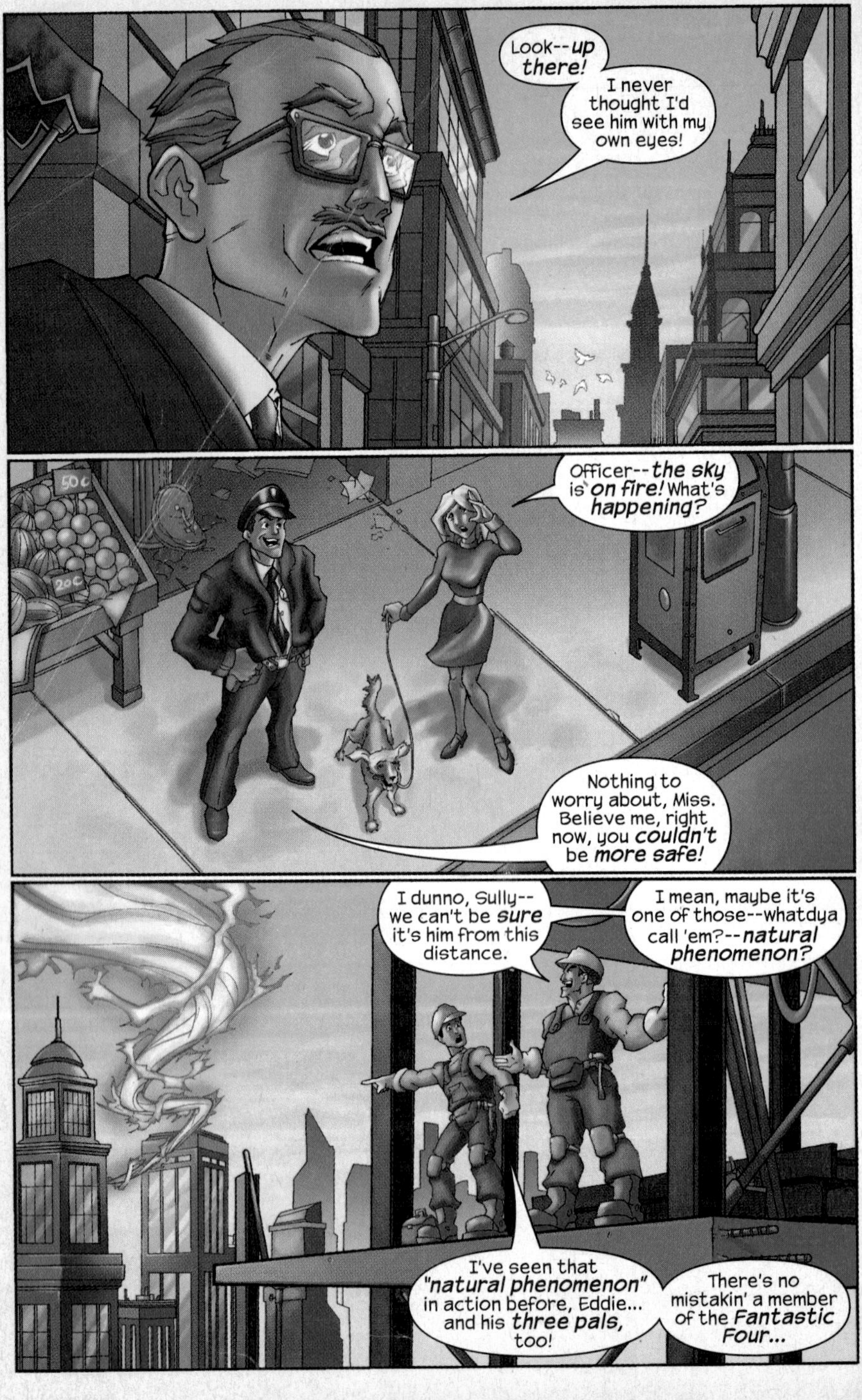
Look--up there!
I never thought I'd see him with my own eyes!
50¢
20¢
Officer--the sky is on fire! What's happening?
Nothing to worry about, Miss. Believe me, right now, you couldn't be more safe!
I dunno, Sully--we can't be sure it's him from this distance.
I mean, maybe it's one of those--whatdya call 'em?--natural phenomenon?
I've seen that "natural phenomenon" in action before, Eddie... and his three pals, too!
There's no mistakin' a member of the Fantastic Four...

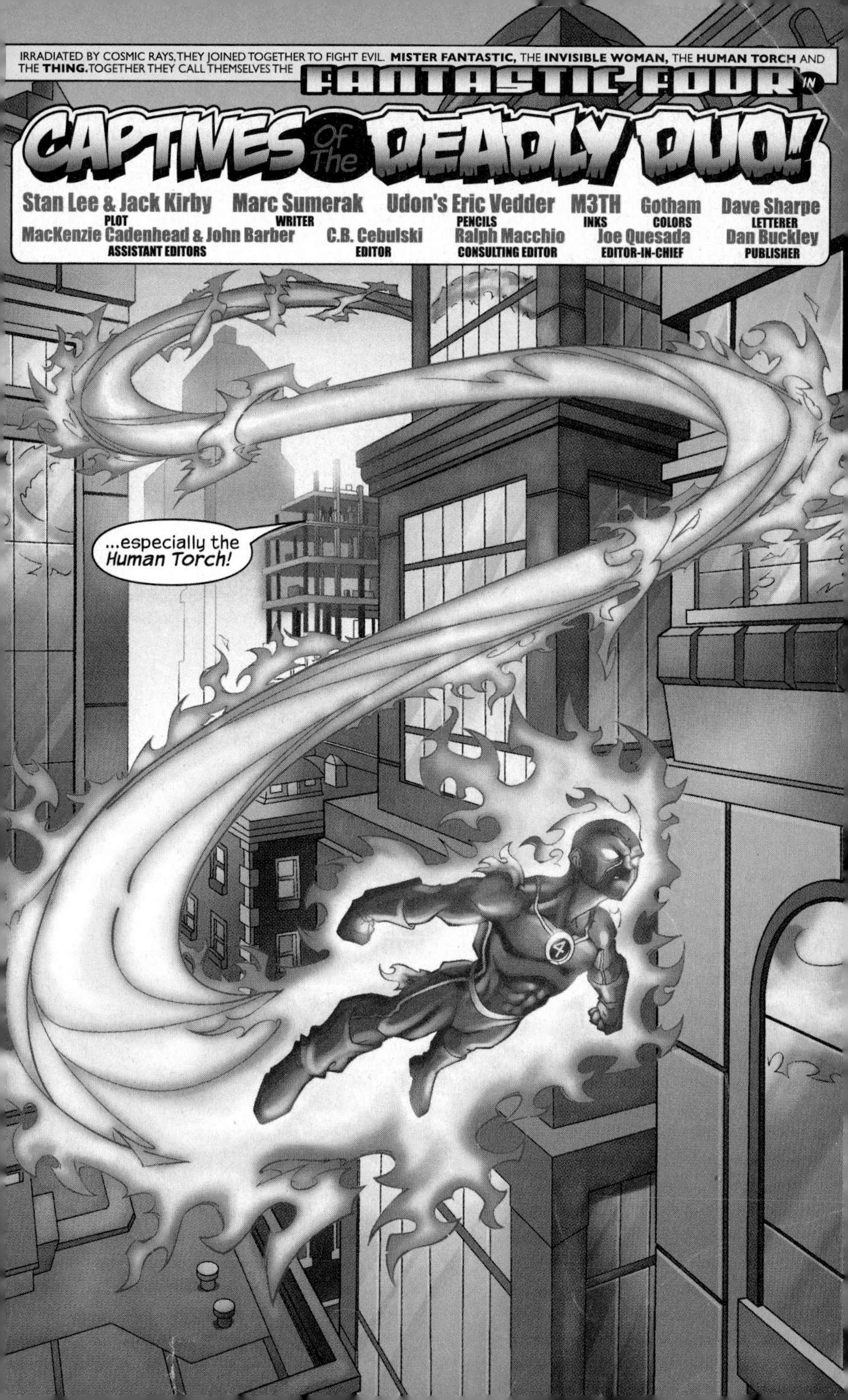
IRRADIATED BY COSMIC RAYS, THEY JOINED TOGETHER TO FIGHT EVIL. MISTER FANTASTIC, THE INVISIBLE WOMAN, THE HUMAN TORCH AND THE THING. TOGETHER THEY CALL THEMSELVES THE
FANTASTIC FOUR IN
CAPTIVES Of The DEADLY DUO!
Stan Lee & Jack Kirby PLOT
Marc Sumerak WRITER
Udon's Eric Vedder PENCILS
M3TH INKS
Gotham COLORS
Dave Sharpe LETTERER
MacKenzie Cadenhead & John Barber ASSISTANT EDITORS
C.B. Cebulski EDITOR
Ralph Macchio CONSULTING EDITOR
Joe Quesada EDITOR-IN-CHIEF
Dan Buckley PUBLISHER
...especially the Human Torch!

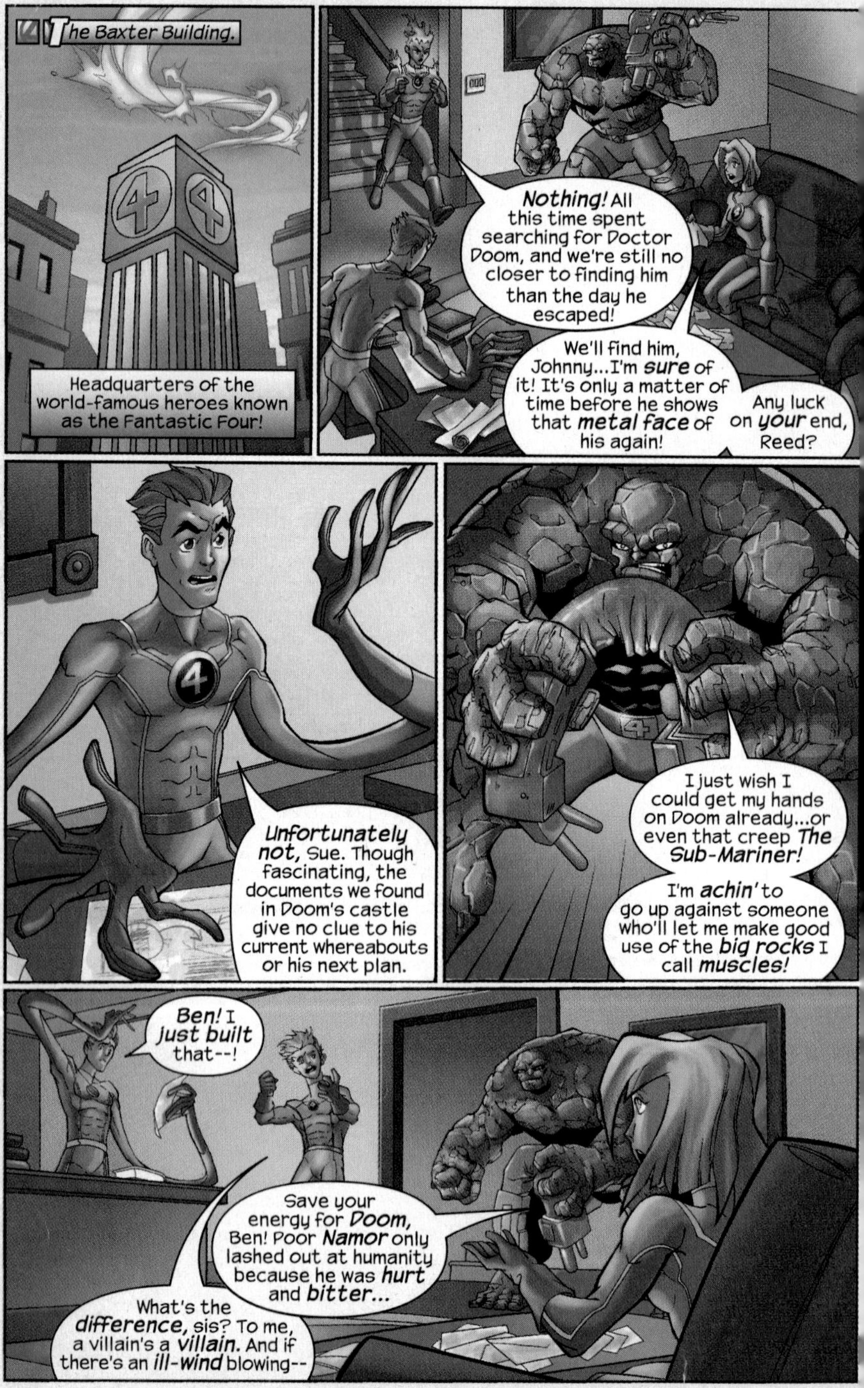
The Baxter Building.
Headquarters of the world-famous heroes known as the Fantastic Four!
Nothing! All this time spent searching for Doctor Doom, and we're still no closer to finding him than the day he escaped!
We'll find him, Johnny...I'm sure of it! It's only a matter of time before he shows that metal face of his again!
Any luck on your end, Reed?
Unfortunately not, Sue. Though fascinating, the documents we found in Doom's castle give no clue to his current whereabouts or his next plan.
I just wish I could get my hands on Doom already...or even that creep The Sub-Mariner!
I'm achin' to go up against someone who'll let me make good use of the big rocks I call muscles!
Ben! I just built that--!
Save your energy for Doom, Ben! Poor Namor only lashed out at humanity because he was hurt and bitter...
What's the difference, sis? To me, a villain's a villain. And if there's an ill-wind blowing--

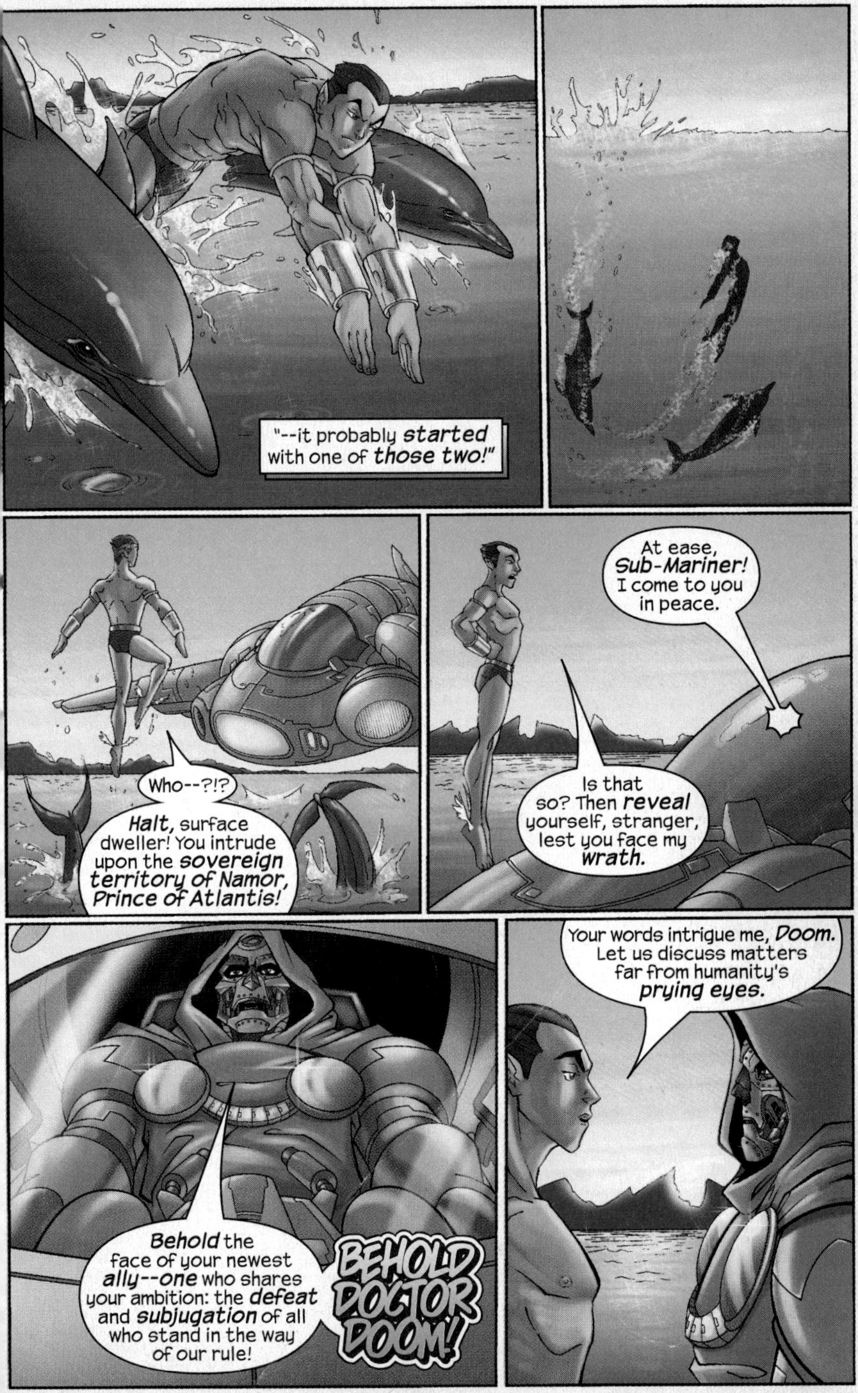
"--it probably started with one of those two!"
Who--?!?
Halt, surface dweller! You intrude upon the sovereign territory of Namor, Prince of Atlantis!
At ease, Sub-Mariner! I come to you in peace.
Is that so? Then reveal yourself, stranger, lest you face my wrath.
Behold the face of your newest ally--one who shares your ambition: the defeat and subjugation of all who stand in the way of our rule!
BEHOLD DOCTOR DOOM!
Your words intrigue me, Doom. Let us discuss matters far from humanity's prying eyes.

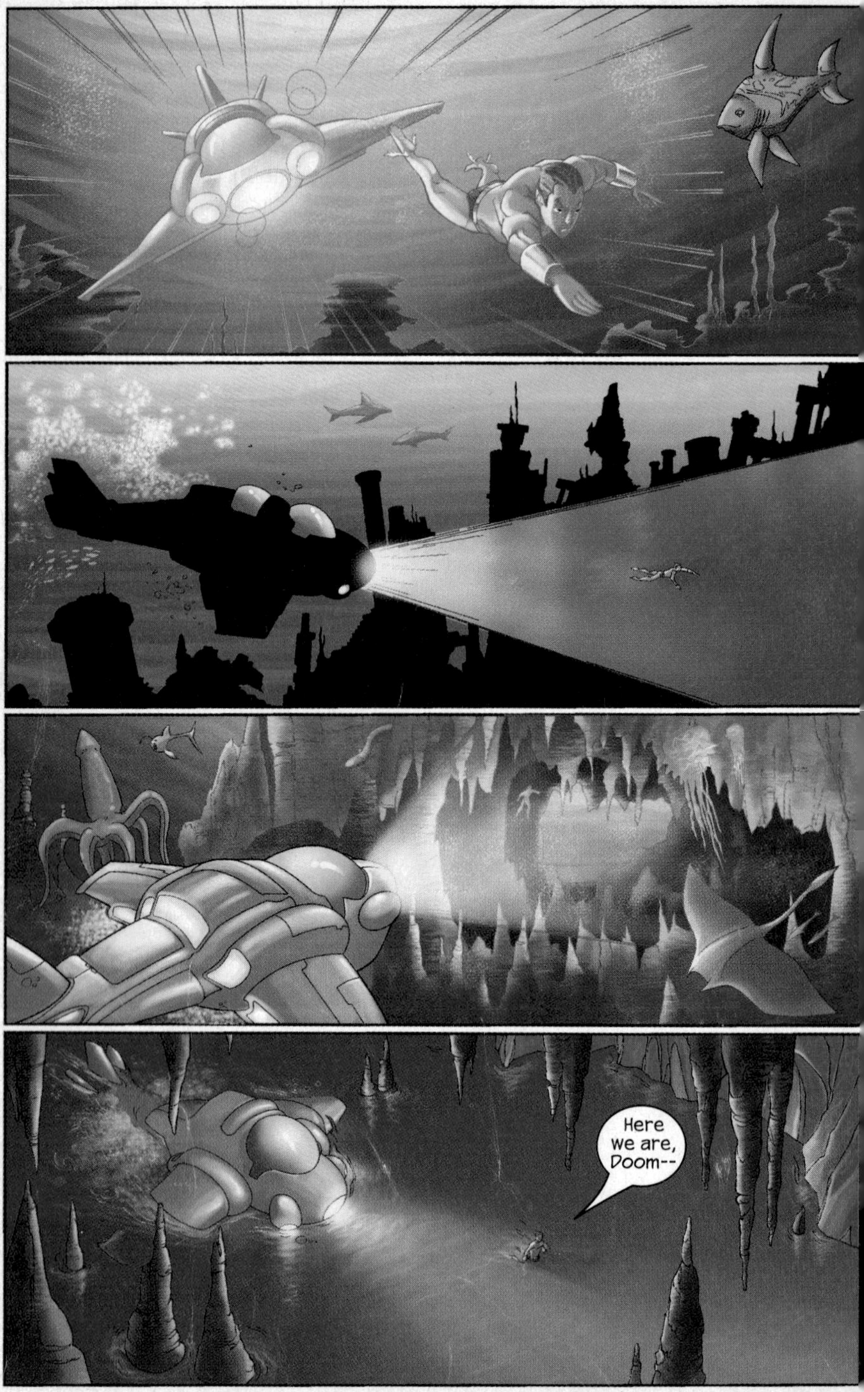
Here we are, Doom--

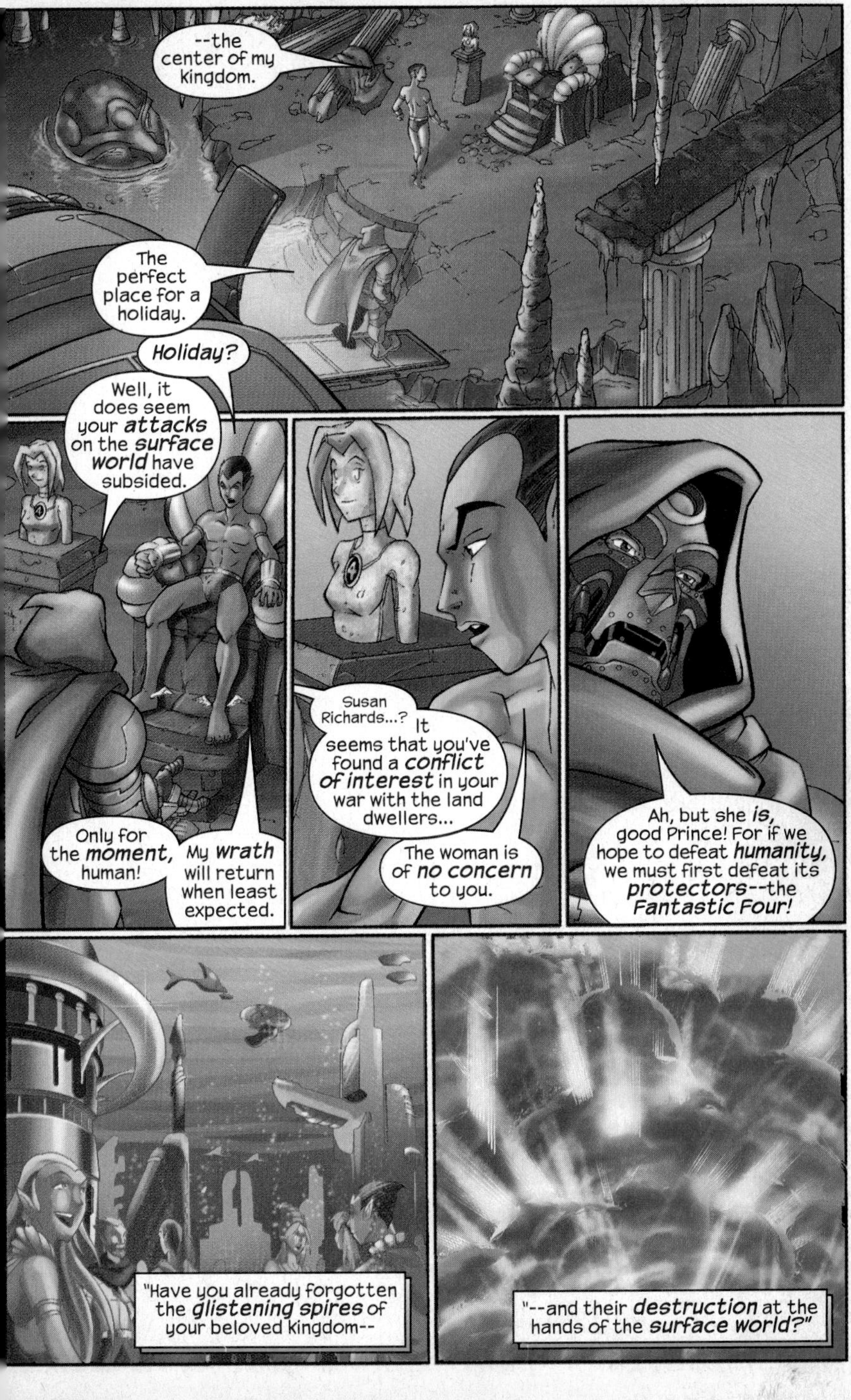
--the center of my kingdom.
The perfect place for a holiday.
Holiday?
Well, it does seem your *attacks* on the *surface world* have subsided.
Only for the *moment,* human!
My *wrath* will return when least expected.
Susan Richards...? It seems that you've found a *conflict of interest* in your war with the land dwellers...
The woman is of *no concern* to you.
Ah, but she *is,* good Prince! For if we hope to defeat *humanity,* we must first defeat its *protectors*--the *Fantastic Four!*
"Have you already forgotten the *glistening spires* of your beloved kingdom--
"--and their *destruction* at the hands of the *surface world?*"

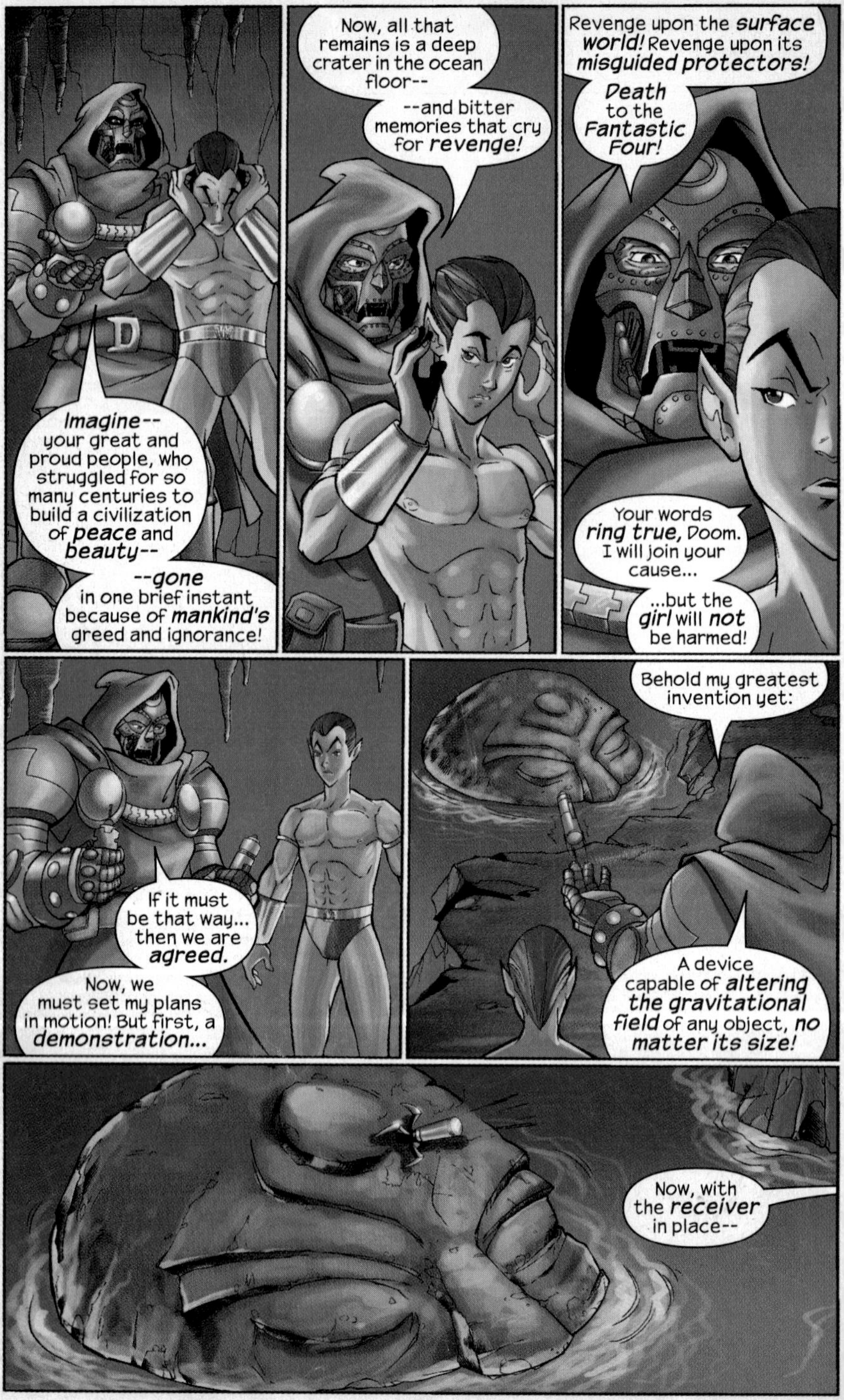
Imagine-- your great and proud people, who struggled for so many centuries to build a civilization of peace and beauty--
--gone in one brief instant because of mankind's greed and ignorance!
Now, all that remains is a deep crater in the ocean floor--
--and bitter memories that cry for revenge!
Revenge upon the surface world! Revenge upon its misguided protectors!
Death to the Fantastic Four!
Your words ring true, Doom. I will join your cause...
...but the girl will not be harmed!
If it must be that way... then we are agreed.
Now, we must set my plans in motion! But first, a demonstration...
Behold my greatest invention yet:
A device capable of altering the gravitational field of any object, no matter its size!
Now, with the receiver in place--

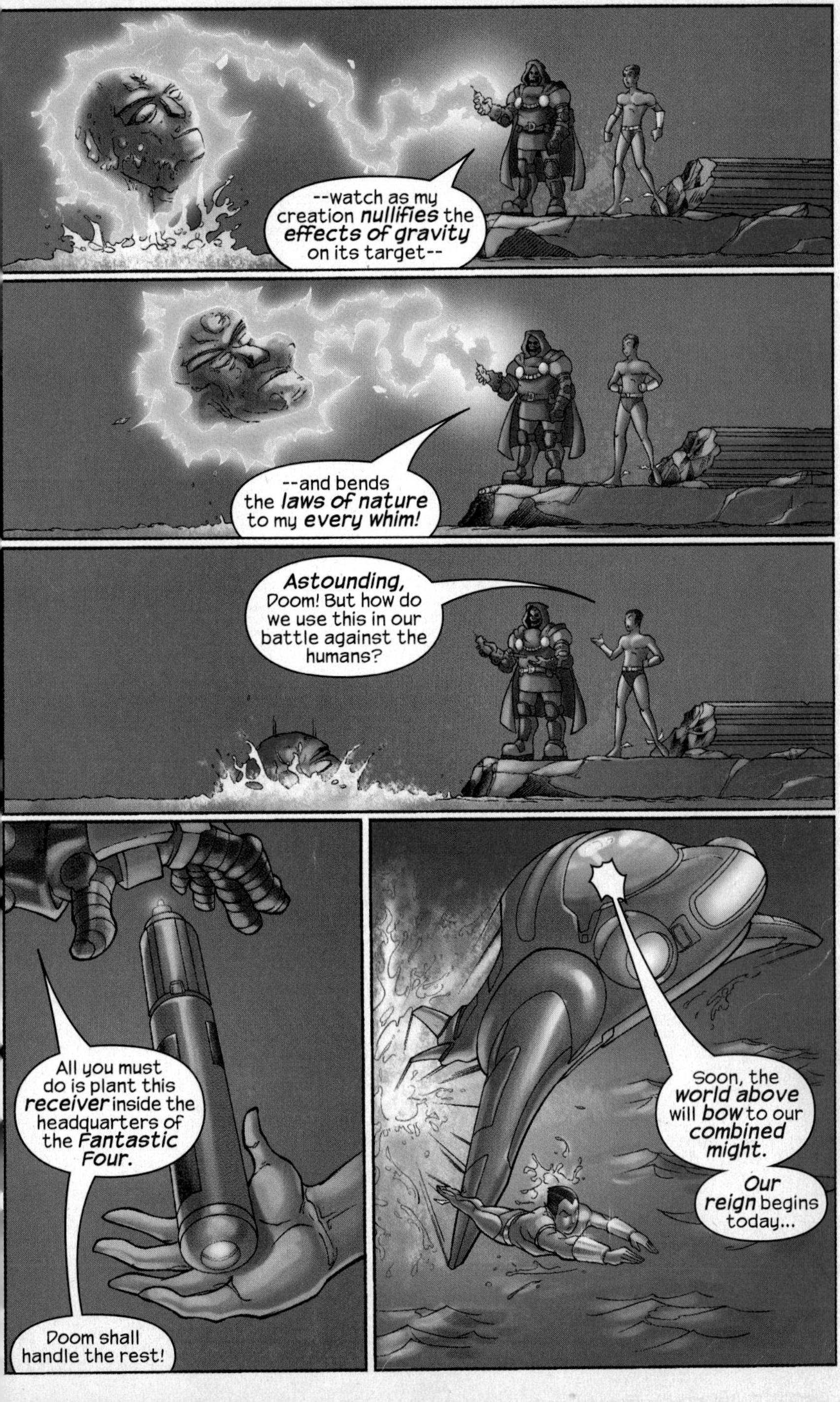
--watch as my creation nullifies the effects of gravity on its target--
--and bends the laws of nature to my every whim!
Astounding, Doom! But how do we use this in our battle against the humans?
All you must do is plant this receiver inside the headquarters of the Fantastic Four.
Doom shall handle the rest!
Soon, the world above will bow to our combined might.
Our reign begins today...

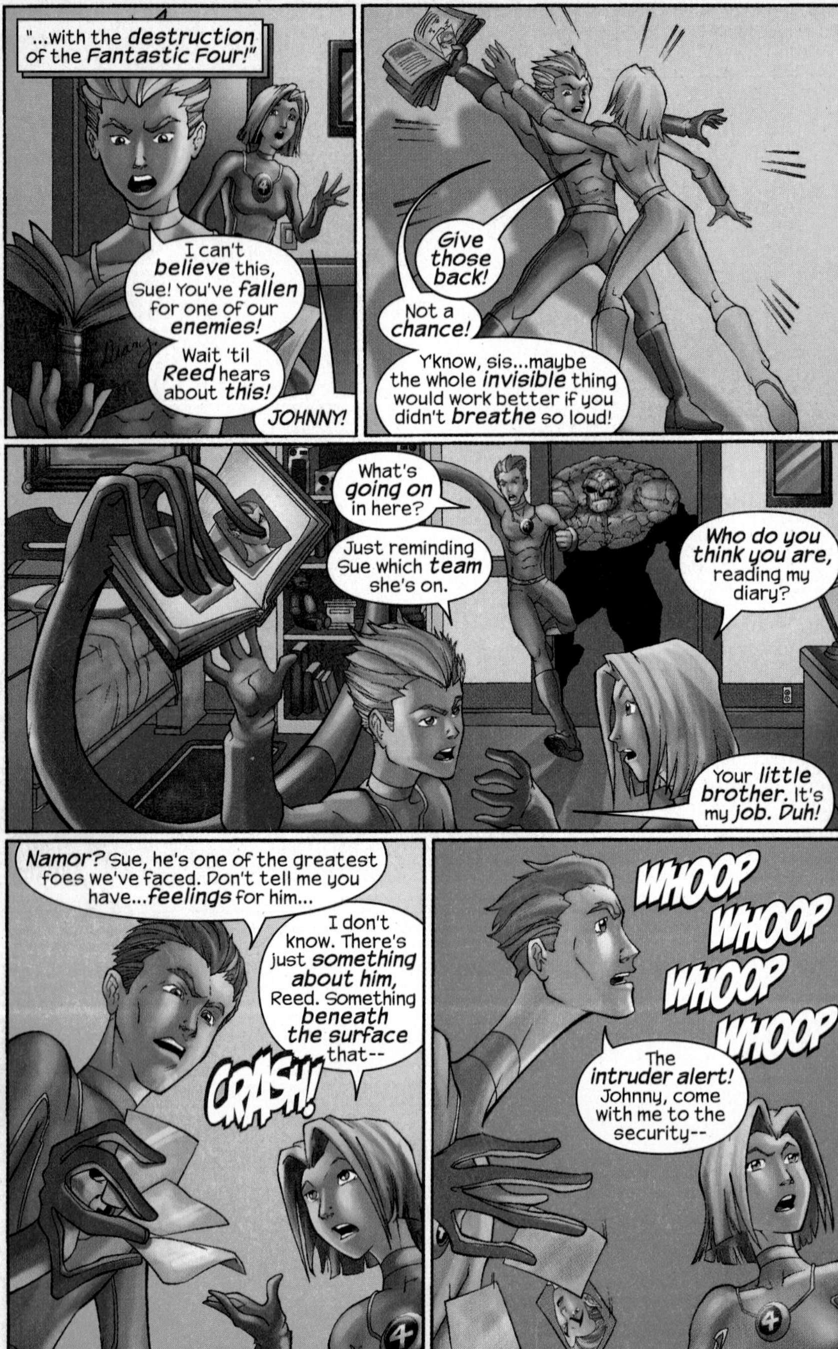
"...with the destruction of the Fantastic Four!"
I can't believe this, Sue! You've fallen for one of our enemies!
Wait 'til Reed hears about this!
JOHNNY!
Give those back!
Not a chance!
Y'know, sis...maybe the whole invisible thing would work better if you didn't breathe so loud!
What's going on in here?
Just reminding Sue which team she's on.
Who do you think you are, reading my diary?
Your little brother. It's my job. Duh!
Namor? Sue, he's one of the greatest foes we've faced. Don't tell me you have...feelings for him...
I don't know. There's just something about him, Reed. Something beneath the surface that--
CRASH!
WHOOP WHOOP WHOOP WHOOP
The intruder alert! Johnny, come with me to the security--

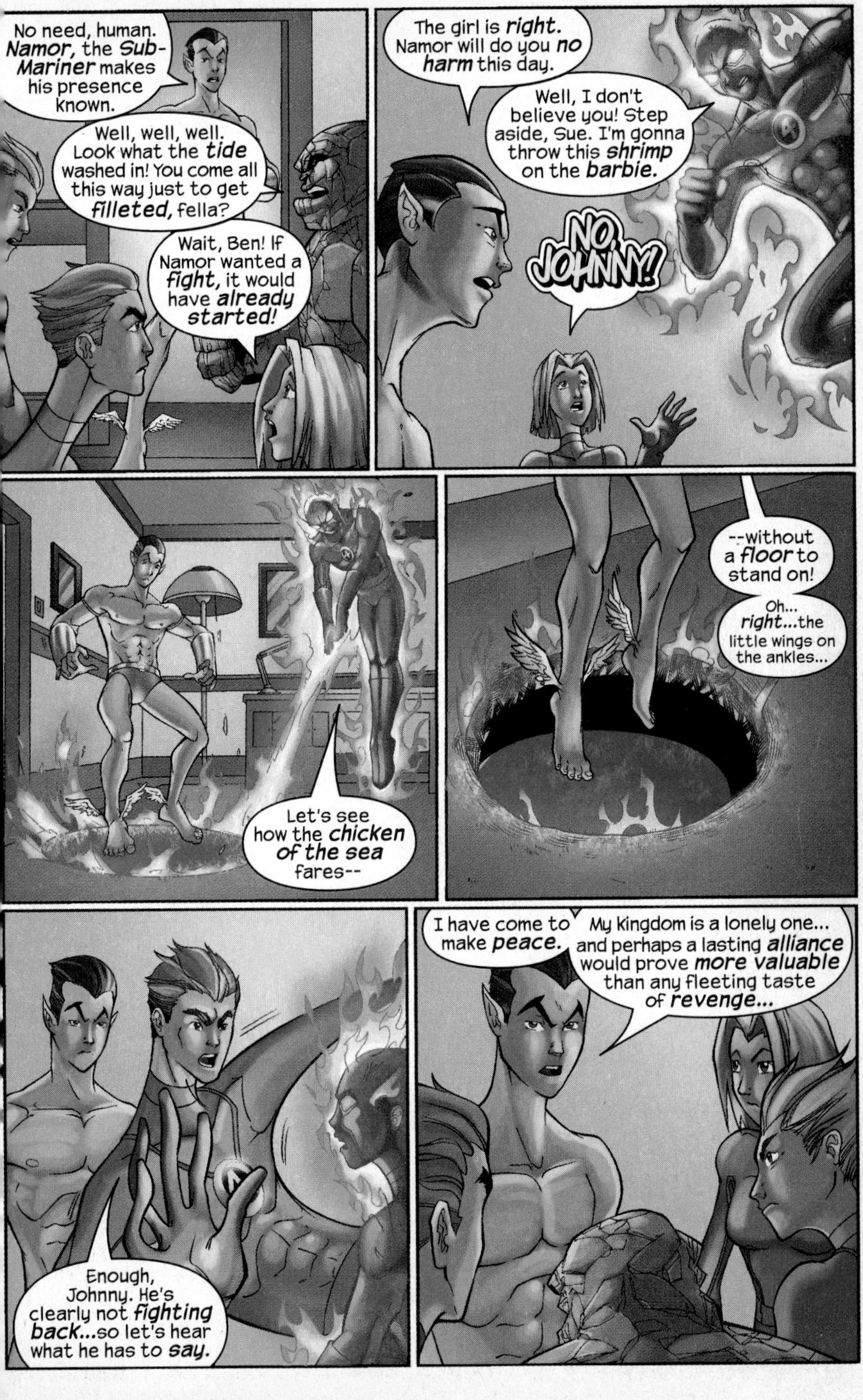
No need, human. Namor, the Sub-Mariner makes his presence known.
Well, well, well. Look what the tide washed in! You come all this way just to get filleted, fella?
Wait, Ben! If Namor wanted a fight, it would have already started!
The girl is right. Namor will do you no harm this day.
Well, I don't believe you! Step aside, Sue. I'm gonna throw this shrimp on the barbie.
NO, JOHNNY!
Let's see how the chicken of the sea fares--
--without a floor to stand on!
Oh... right...the little wings on the ankles...
Enough, Johnny. He's clearly not fighting back...so let's hear what he has to say.
I have come to make peace.
My kingdom is a lonely one... and perhaps a lasting alliance would prove more valuable than any fleeting taste of revenge...

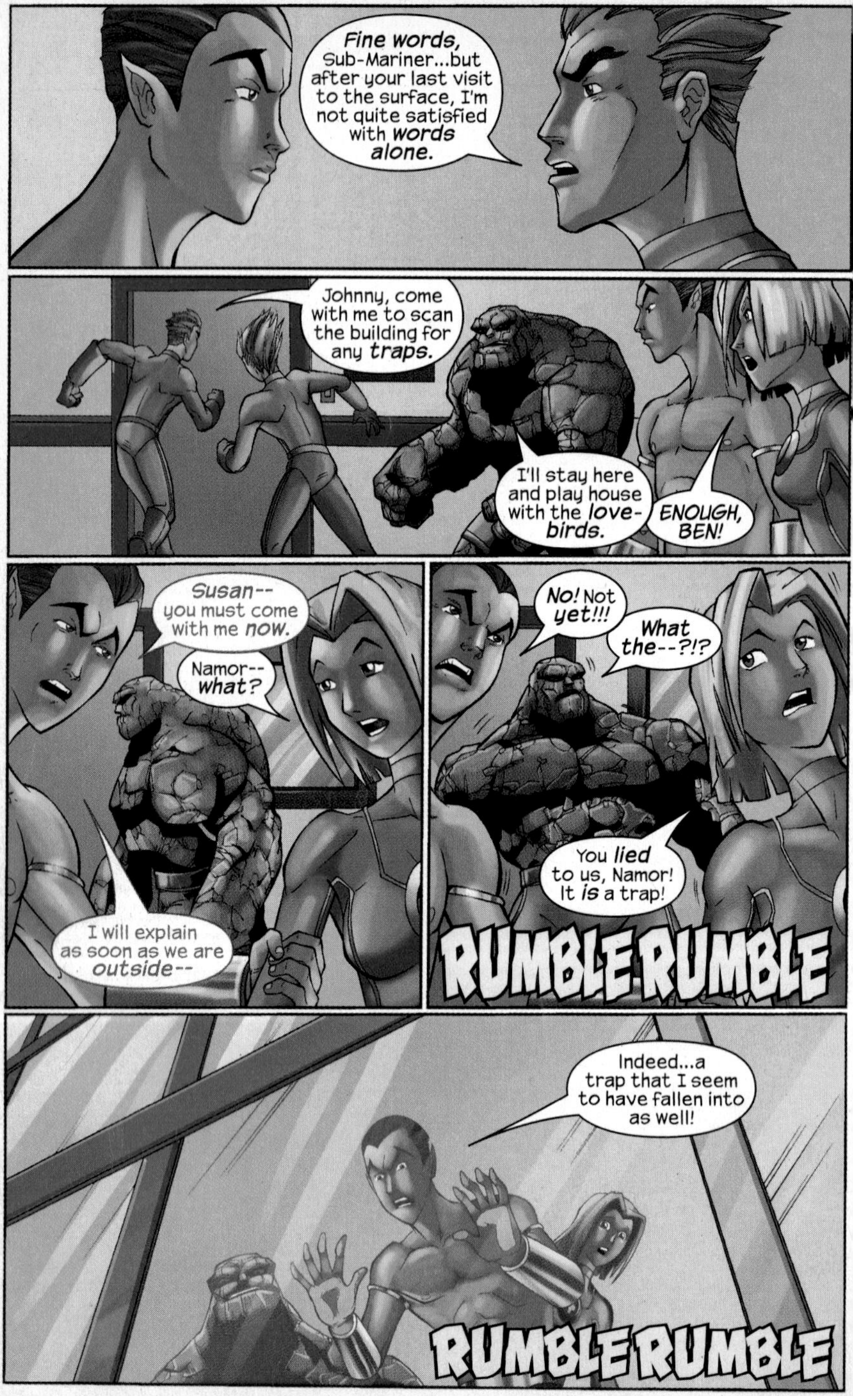

Fine words, Sub-Mariner...but after your last visit to the surface, I'm not quite satisfied with words alone.
Johnny, come with me to scan the building for any traps.
I'll stay here and play house with the love-birds.
ENOUGH, BEN!
Susan-- you must come with me now.
Namor-- what?
I will explain as soon as we are outside--
No! Not yet!!!
What the--?!?
You lied to us, Namor! It is a trap!
RUMBLE RUMBLE
Indeed...a trap that I seem to have fallen into as well!
RUMBLE RUMBLE

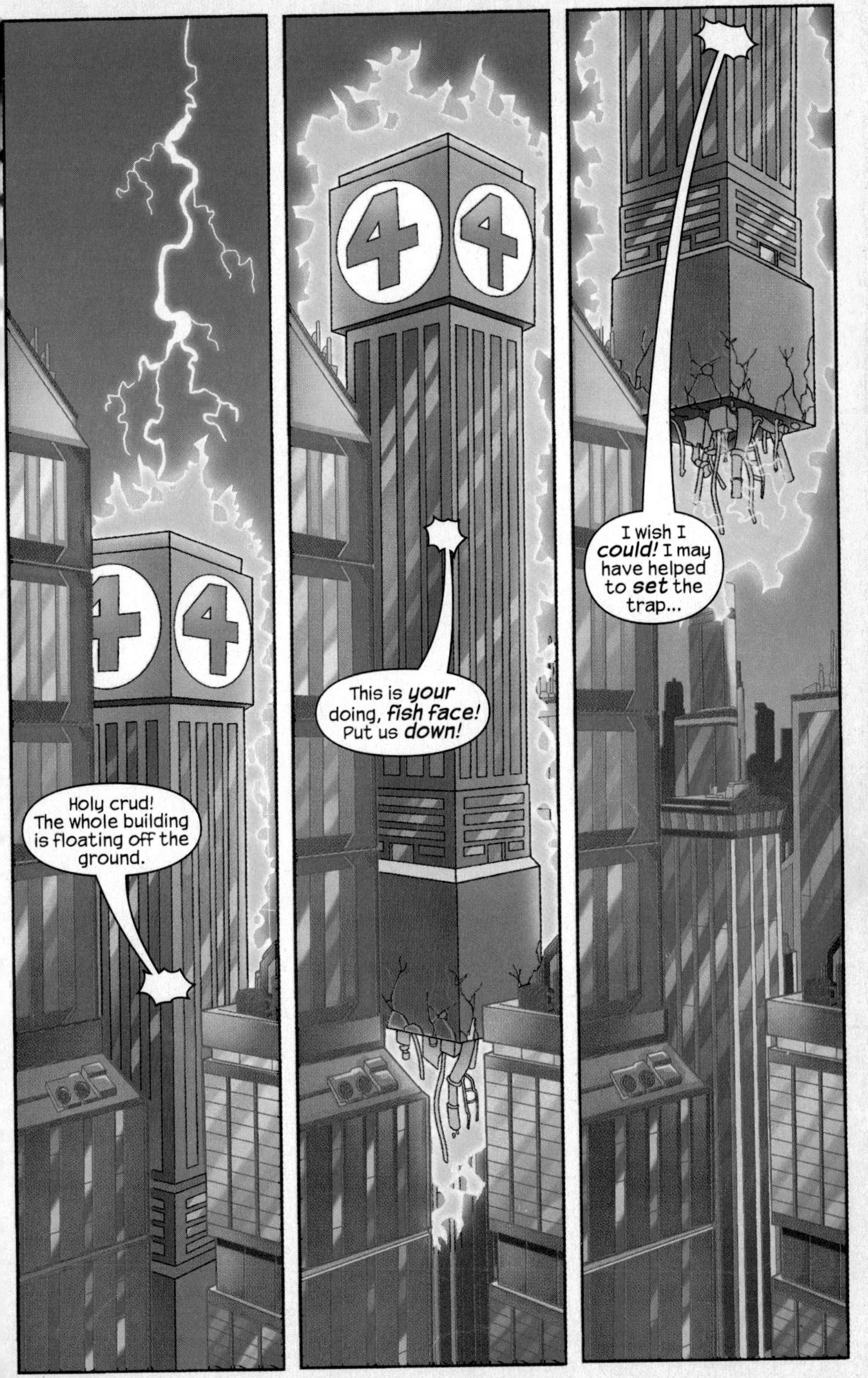
Holy crud! The whole building is floating off the ground.
This is *your* doing, *fish face!* Put us *down!*
I wish I *could!* I may have helped to *set* the trap...

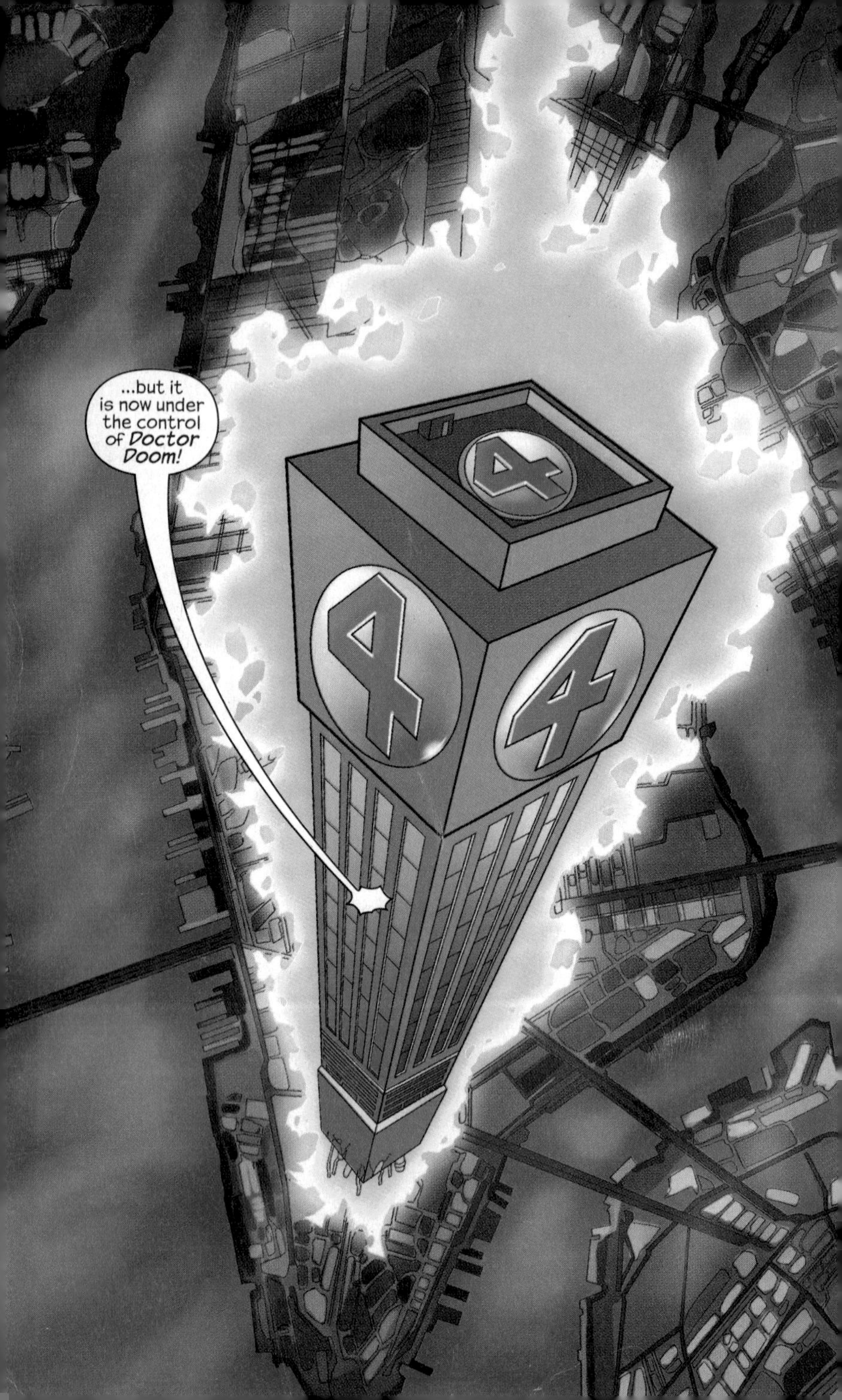
...but it is now under the control of *Doctor Doom!*

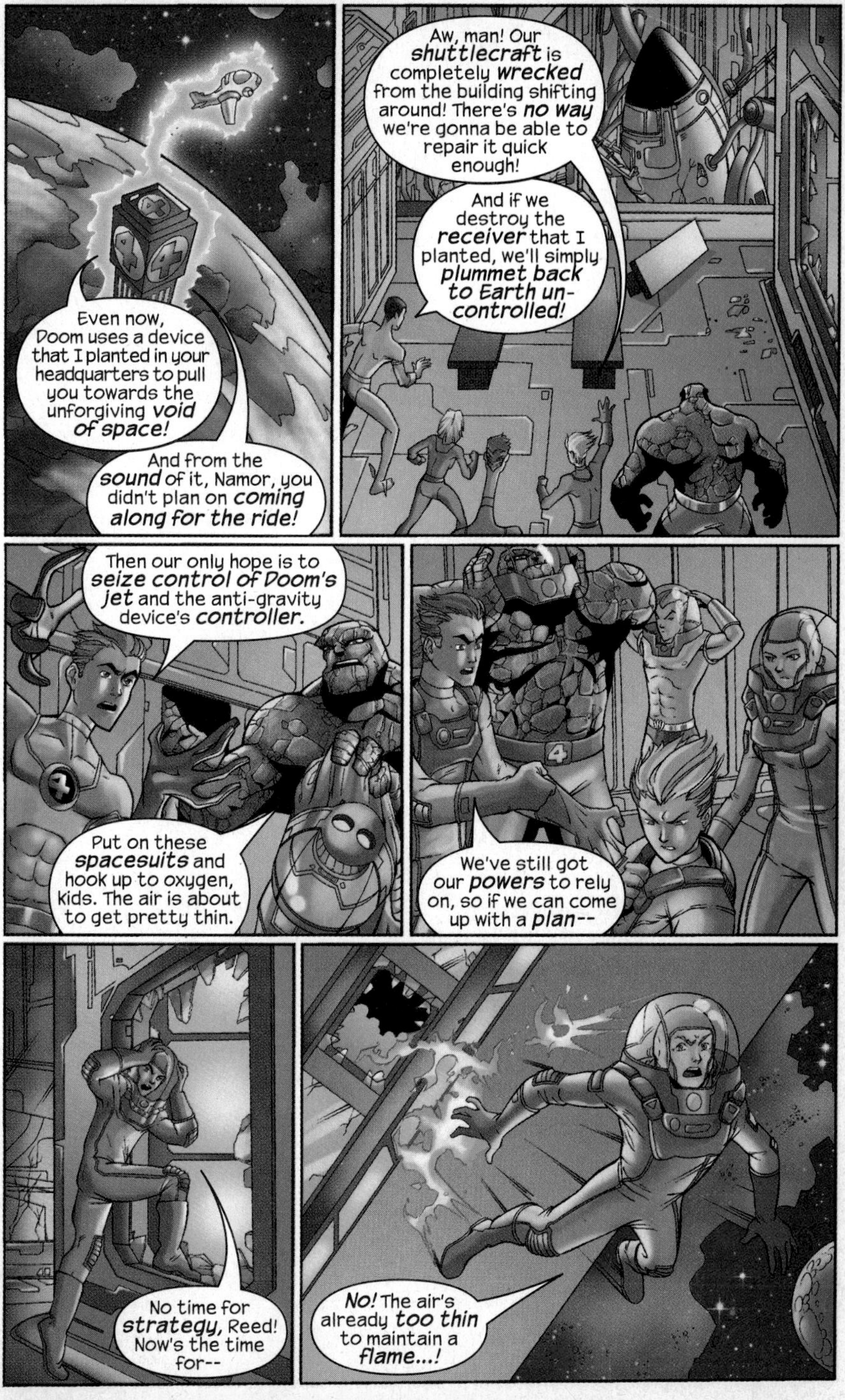
Even now, Doom uses a device that I planted in your headquarters to pull you towards the unforgiving void of space!
And from the sound of it, Namor, you didn't plan on coming along for the ride!
Aw, man! Our shuttlecraft is completely wrecked from the building shifting around! There's no way we're gonna be able to repair it quick enough!
And if we destroy the receiver that I planted, we'll simply plummet back to Earth un-controlled!
Then our only hope is to seize control of Doom's jet and the anti-gravity device's controller.
Put on these spacesuits and hook up to oxygen, kids. The air is about to get pretty thin.
We've still got our powers to rely on, so if we can come up with a plan--
No time for strategy, Reed! Now's the time for--
No! The air's already too thin to maintain a flame...!

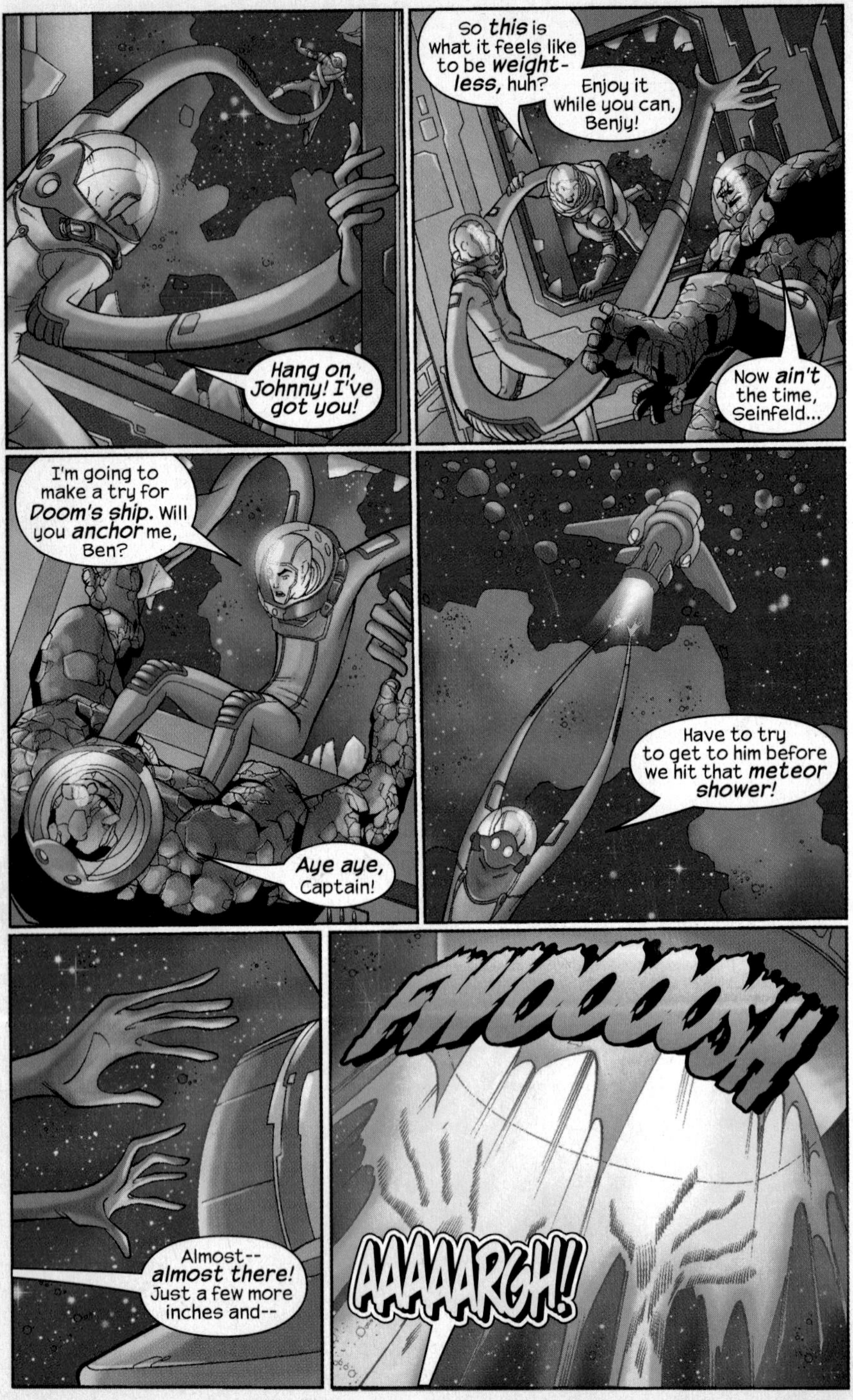
So this is what it feels like to be weight-less, huh?
Enjoy it while you can, Benjy!
Hang on, Johnny! I've got you!
Now ain't the time, Seinfeld...
I'm going to make a try for Doom's ship. Will you anchor me, Ben?
Aye aye, Captain!
Have to try to get to him before we hit that meteor shower!
Almost-- almost there! Just a few more inches and--
FWOOOSH
AAAAARGH!!

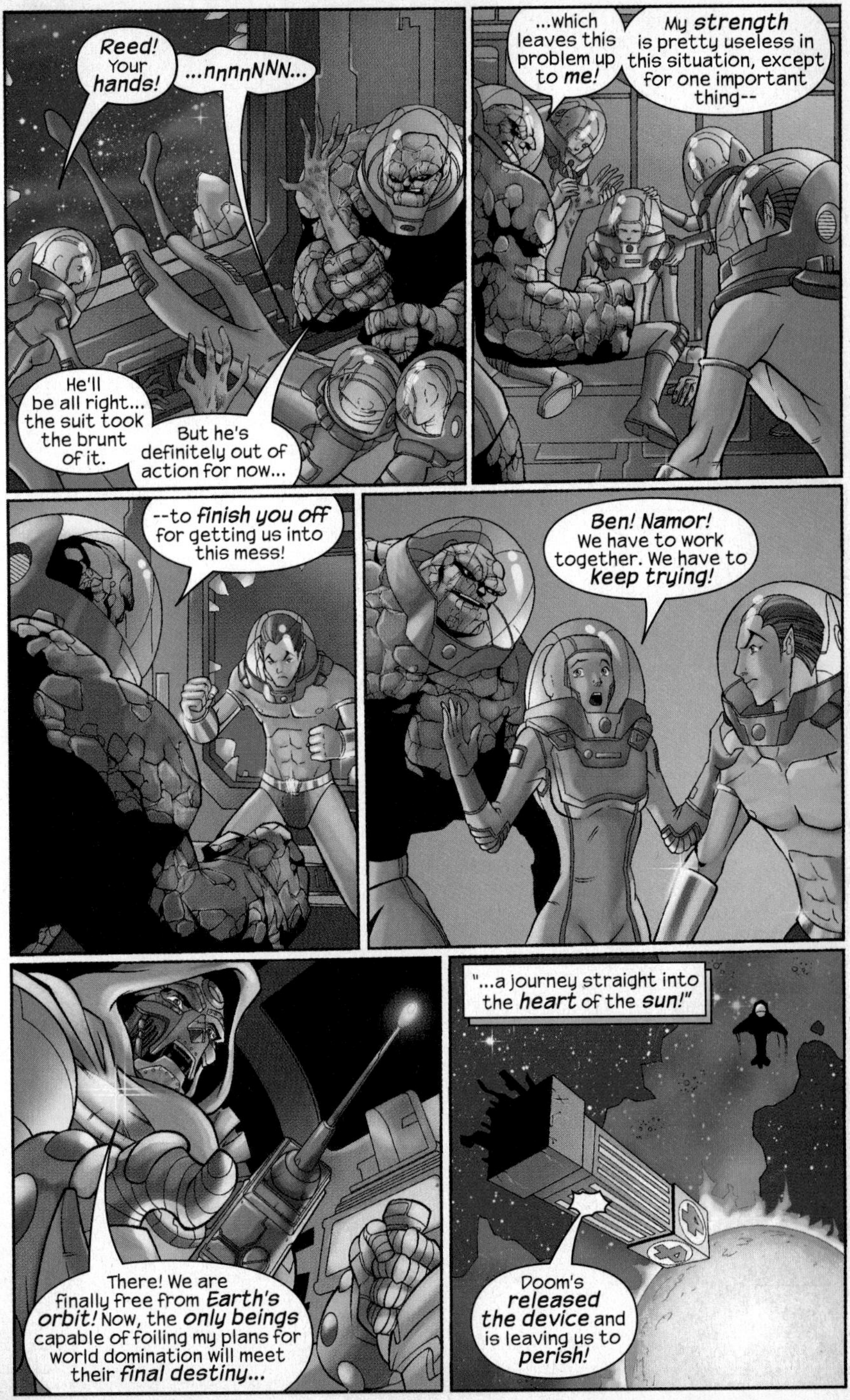

Reed! Your hands!
...nnnnNNN...
He'll be all right... the suit took the brunt of it.
But he's definitely out of action for now...
...which leaves this problem up to me!
My strength is pretty useless in this situation, except for one important thing--
--to finish you off for getting us into this mess!
Ben! Namor! We have to work together. We have to keep trying!
There! We are finally free from Earth's orbit! Now, the only beings capable of foiling my plans for world domination will meet their final destiny...
"...a journey straight into the heart of the sun!"
Doom's released the device and is leaving us to perish!

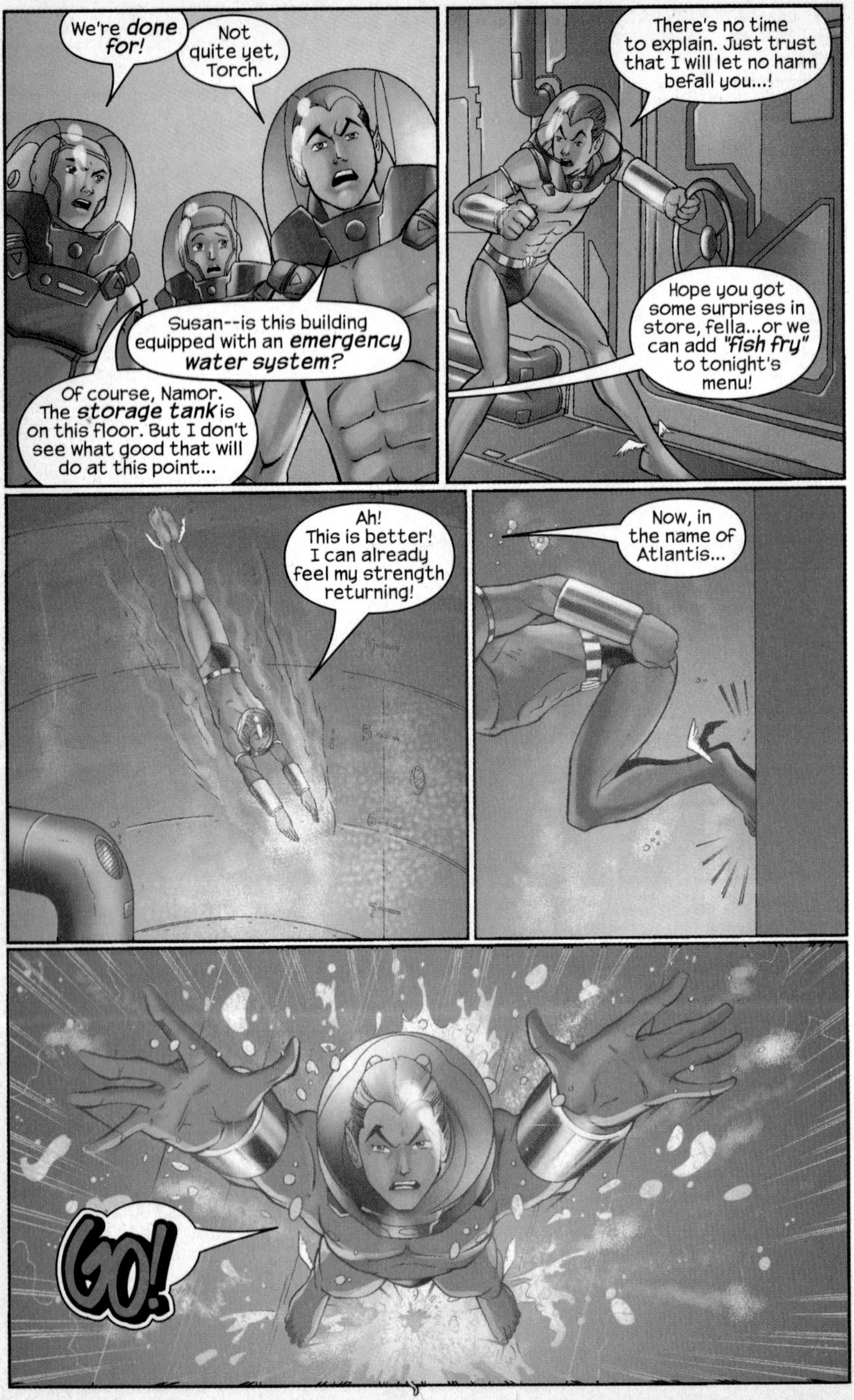
We're done for!
Not quite yet, Torch.
Susan--is this building equipped with an emergency water system?
Of course, Namor. The storage tank is on this floor. But I don't see what good that will do at this point...
There's no time to explain. Just trust that I will let no harm befall you...!
Hope you got some surprises in store, fella...or we can add "fish fry" to tonight's menu!
Ah! This is better! I can already feel my strength returning!
Now, in the name of Atlantis...
GO!

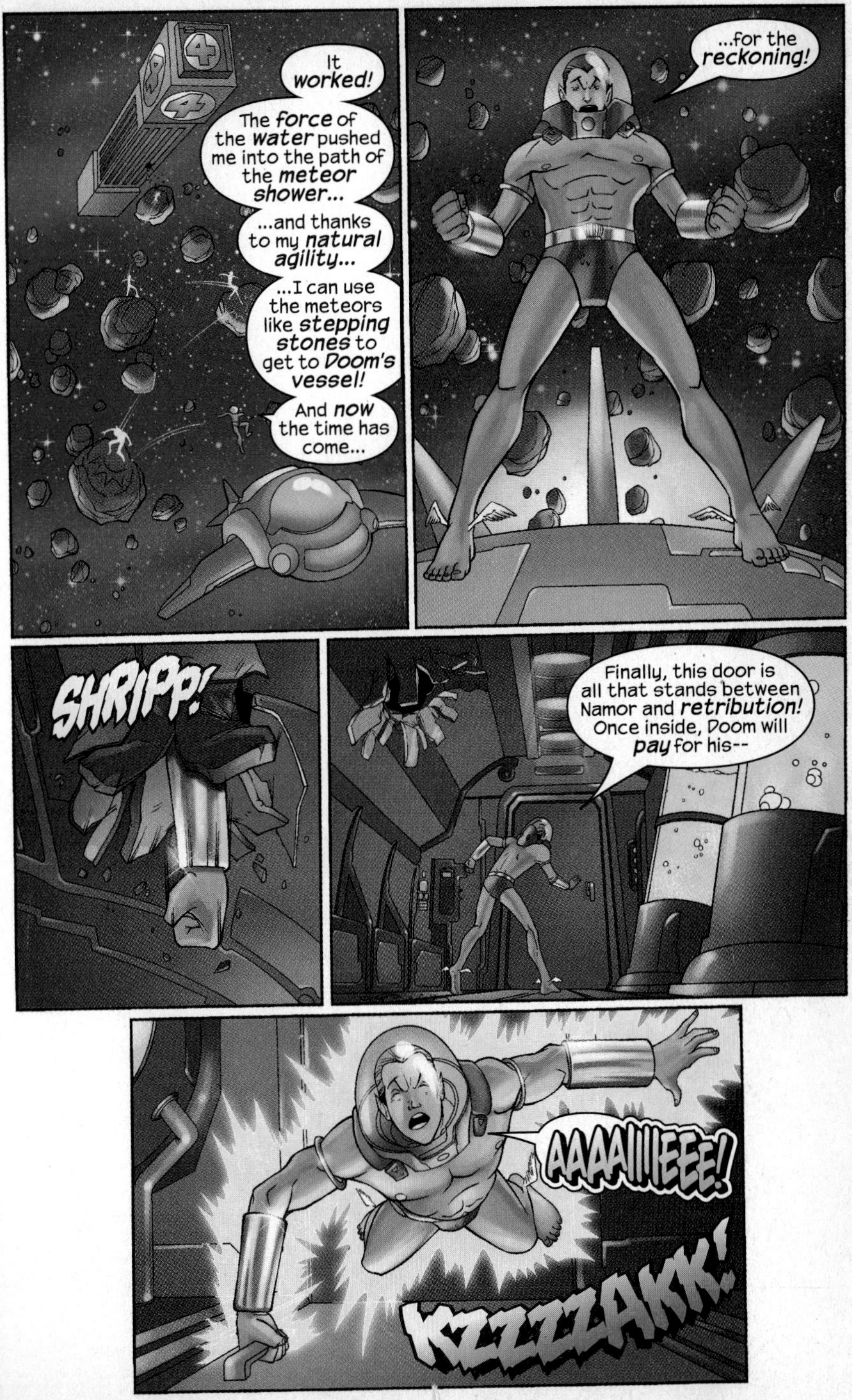

It worked!
The force of the water pushed me into the path of the meteor shower...
...and thanks to my natural agility...
...I can use the meteors like stepping stones to get to Doom's vessel!
And now the time has come...
...for the reckoning!
SHRIPP!
Finally, this door is all that stands between Namor and retribution! Once inside, Doom will pay for his--
AAAAIIIIEEE!
KZZZZAKK!

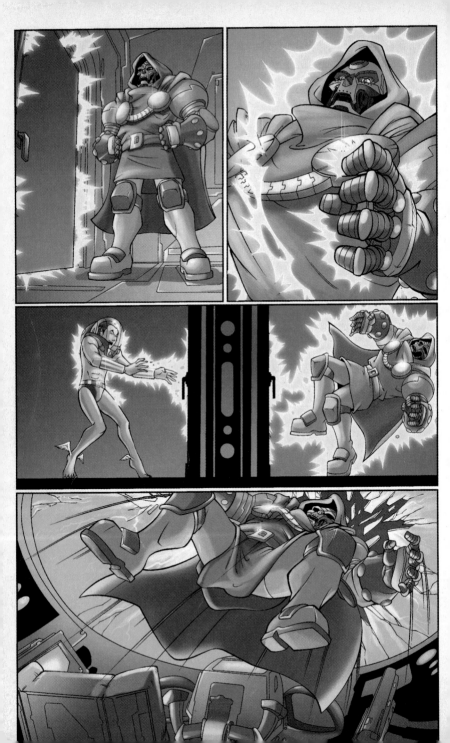

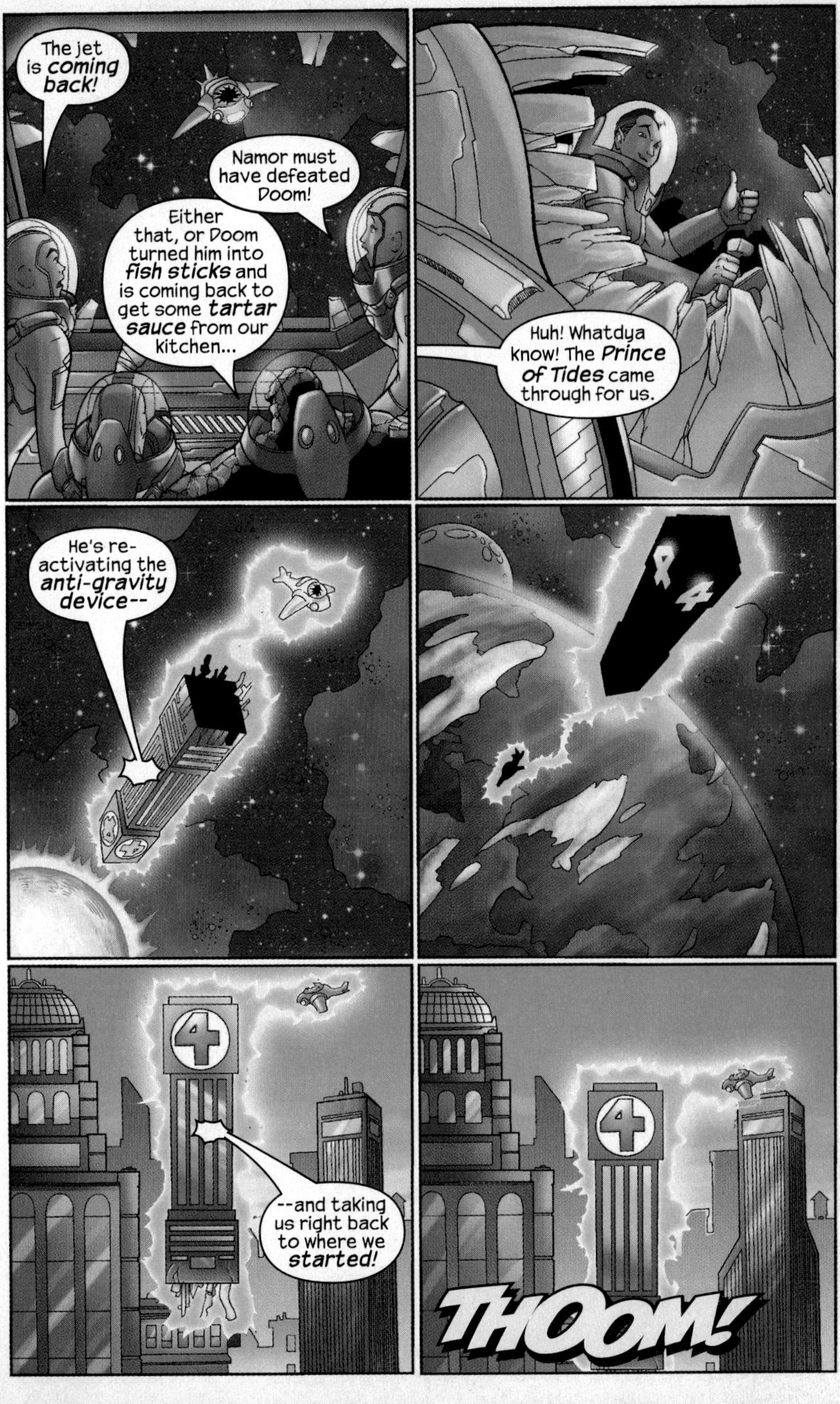
The jet is coming back!
Namor must have defeated Doom!
Either that, or Doom turned him into fish sticks and is coming back to get some tartar sauce from our kitchen...
Huh! Whatdya know! The Prince of Tides came through for us.
He's re-activating the anti-gravity device--
--and taking us right back to where we started!
THOOM!

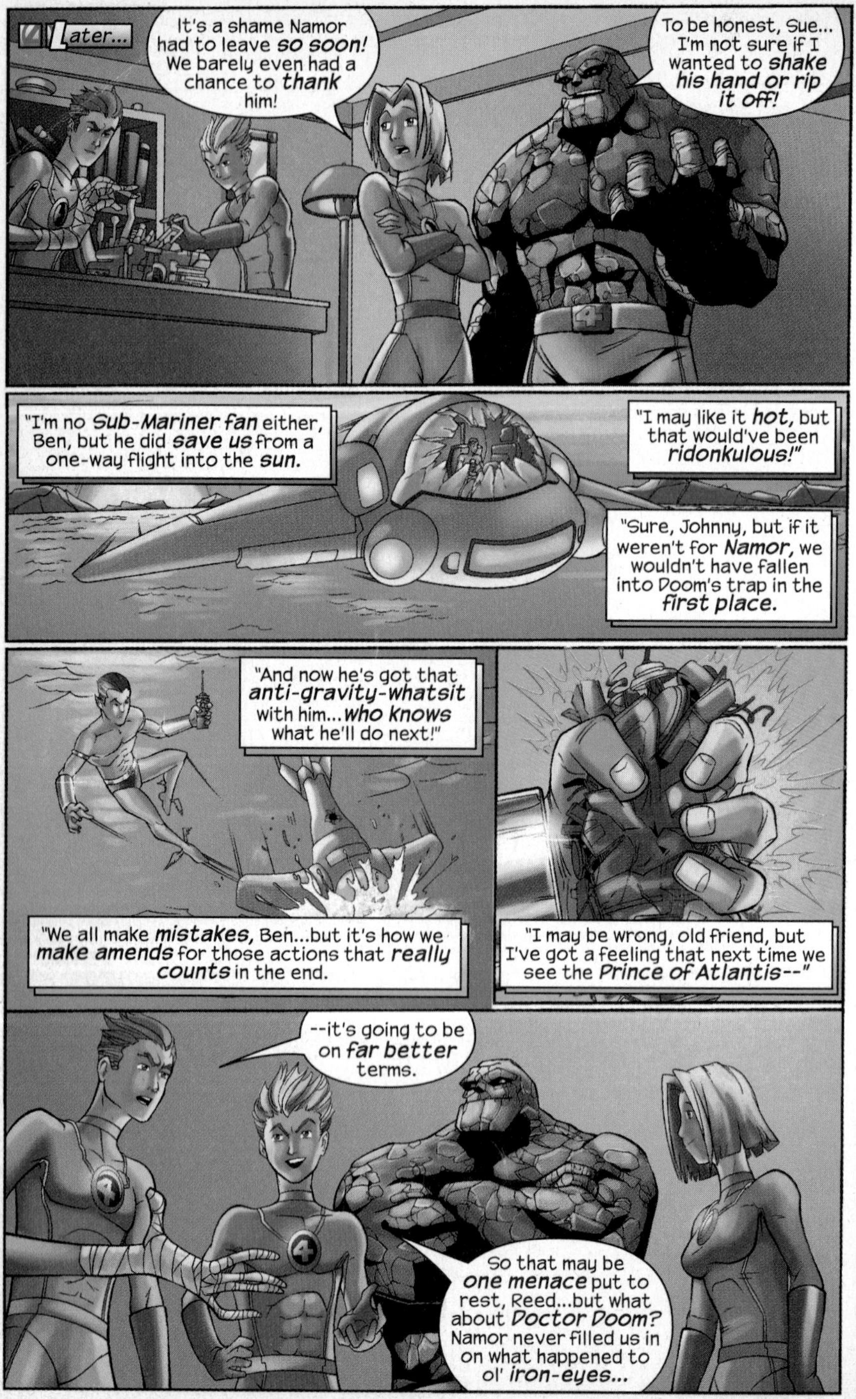
Later...
It's a shame Namor had to leave so soon! We barely even had a chance to thank him!
To be honest, Sue... I'm not sure if I wanted to shake his hand or rip it off!
"I'm no Sub-Mariner fan either, Ben, but he did save us from a one-way flight into the sun.
"I may like it hot, but that would've been ridonkulous!"
"Sure, Johnny, but if it weren't for Namor, we wouldn't have fallen into Doom's trap in the first place.
"And now he's got that anti-gravity-whatsit with him...who knows what he'll do next!"
"We all make mistakes, Ben...but it's how we make amends for those actions that really counts in the end.
"I may be wrong, old friend, but I've got a feeling that next time we see the Prince of Atlantis--"
--it's going to be on far better terms.
So that may be one menace put to rest, Reed...but what about Doctor Doom? Namor never filled us in on what happened to ol' iron-eyes...

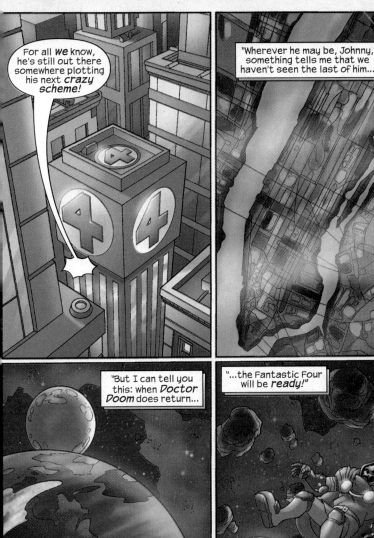

For all *we* know, he's still out there somewhere plotting his next *crazy scheme!*

"Wherever he may be, Johnny, something tells me that we haven't seen the last of him...

"But I can tell you this: when *Doctor Doom* does return...

"...the Fantastic Four will be *ready!*"

The end.

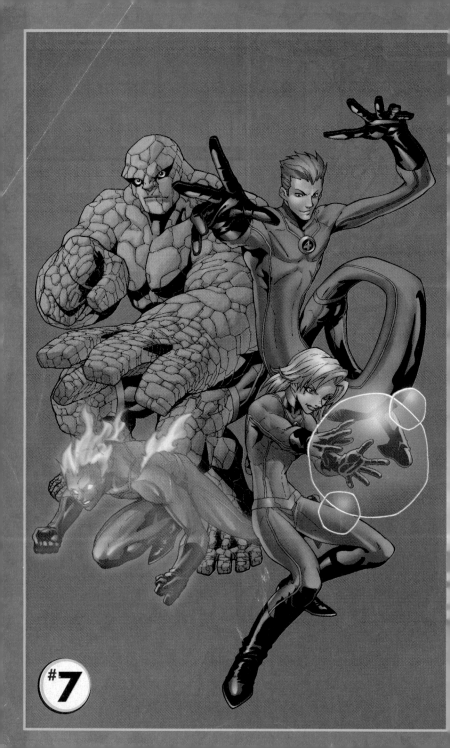

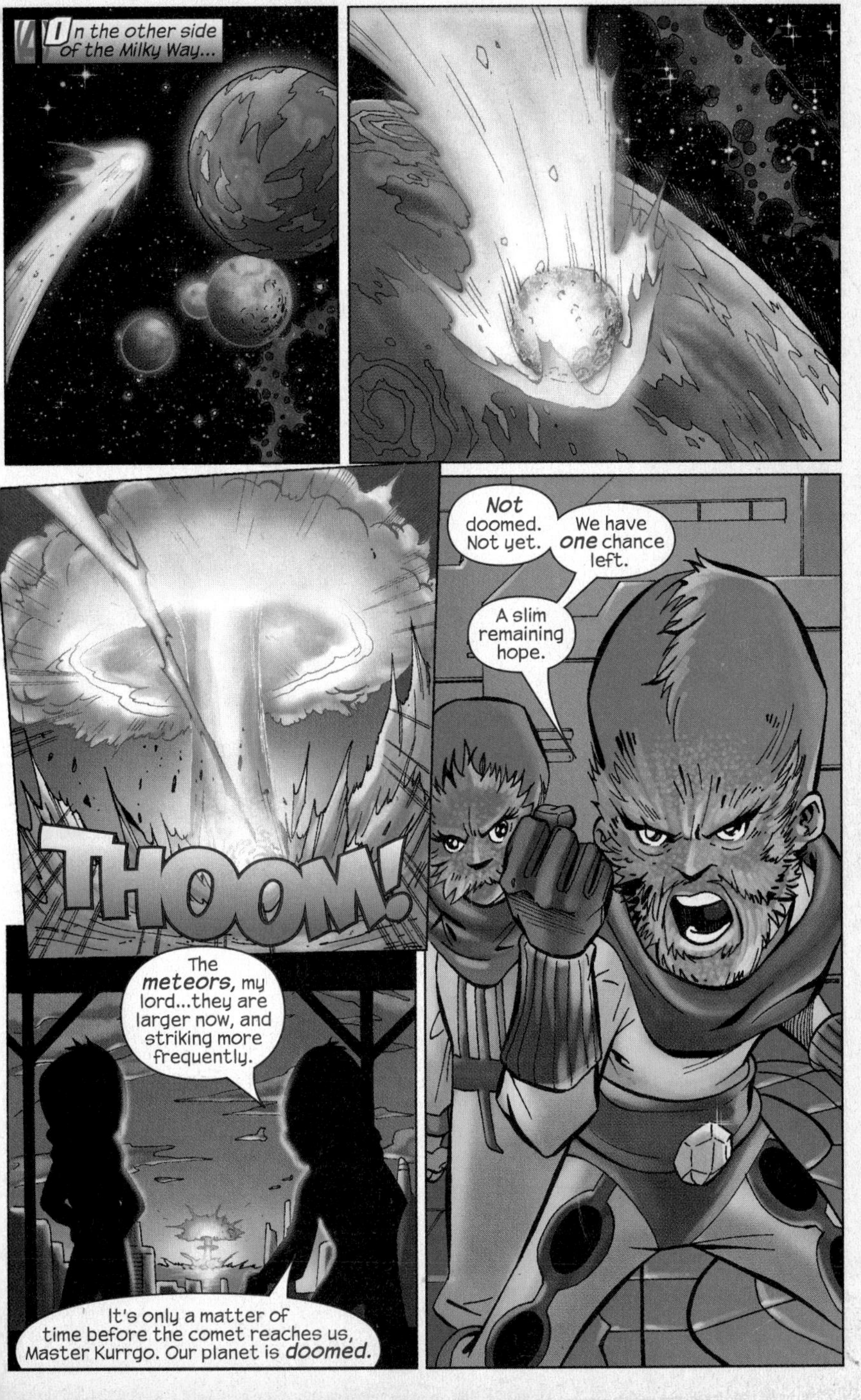
On the other side of the Milky Way...
THOOM!
The meteors, my lord...they are larger now, and striking more frequently.
It's only a matter of time before the comet reaches us, Master Kurrgo. Our planet is doomed.
Not doomed. Not yet.
We have one chance left.
A slim remaining hope.

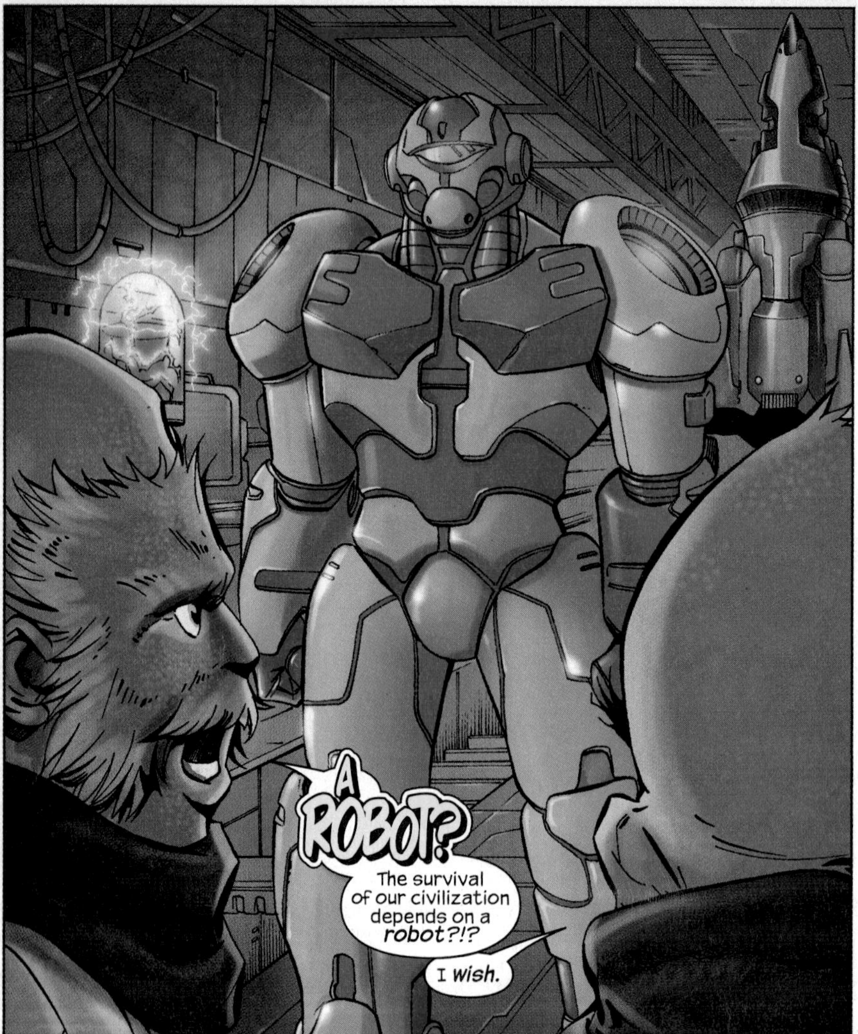
A ROBOT?
The survival of our civilization depends on a *robot*?!?
I *wish*.

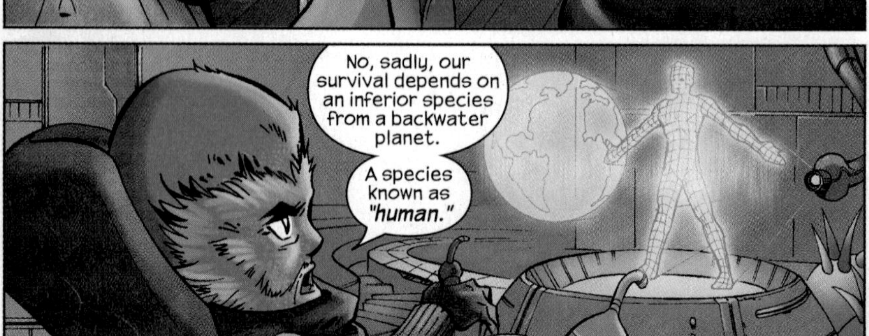
No, sadly, our survival depends on an inferior species from a backwater planet.
A species known as *"human."*

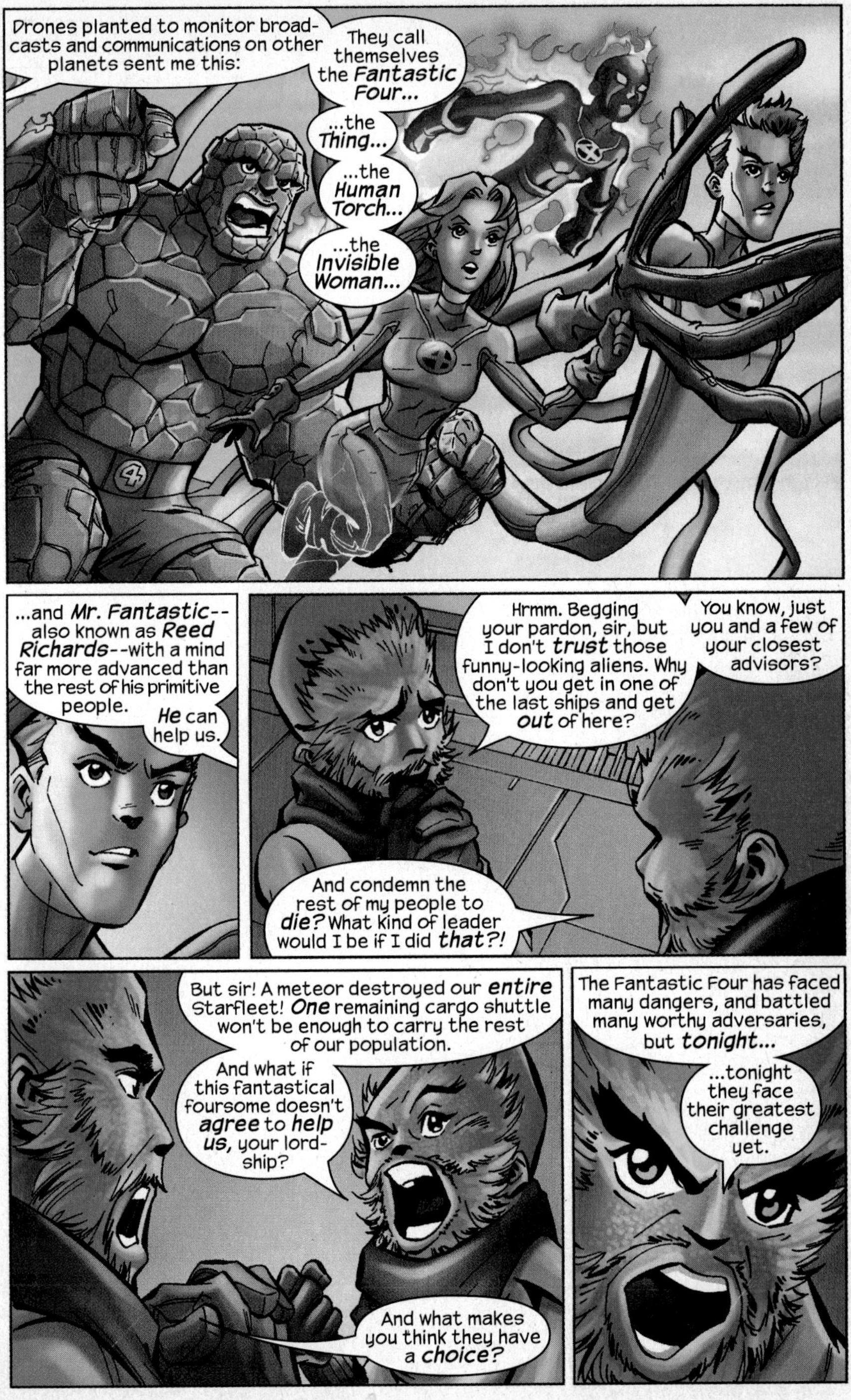
Drones planted to monitor broadcasts and communications on other planets sent me this:
They call themselves the *Fantastic Four...*
...the *Thing...*
...the *Human Torch...*
...the *Invisible Woman...*
...and *Mr. Fantastic*--also known as *Reed Richards*--with a mind far more advanced than the rest of his primitive people.
He can help us.
Hrmm. Begging your pardon, sir, but I don't *trust* those funny-looking aliens. Why don't you get in one of the last ships and get *out* of here?
You know, just you and a few of your closest advisors?
And condemn the rest of my people to *die?* What kind of leader would I be if I did *that?!*
But sir! A meteor destroyed our *entire* Starfleet! *One* remaining cargo shuttle won't be enough to carry the rest of our population.
And what if this fantastical foursome doesn't *agree* to *help us,* your lordship?
And what makes you think they have a *choice?*
The Fantastic Four has faced many dangers, and battled many worthy adversaries, but *tonight...*
...tonight they face their greatest challenge yet.

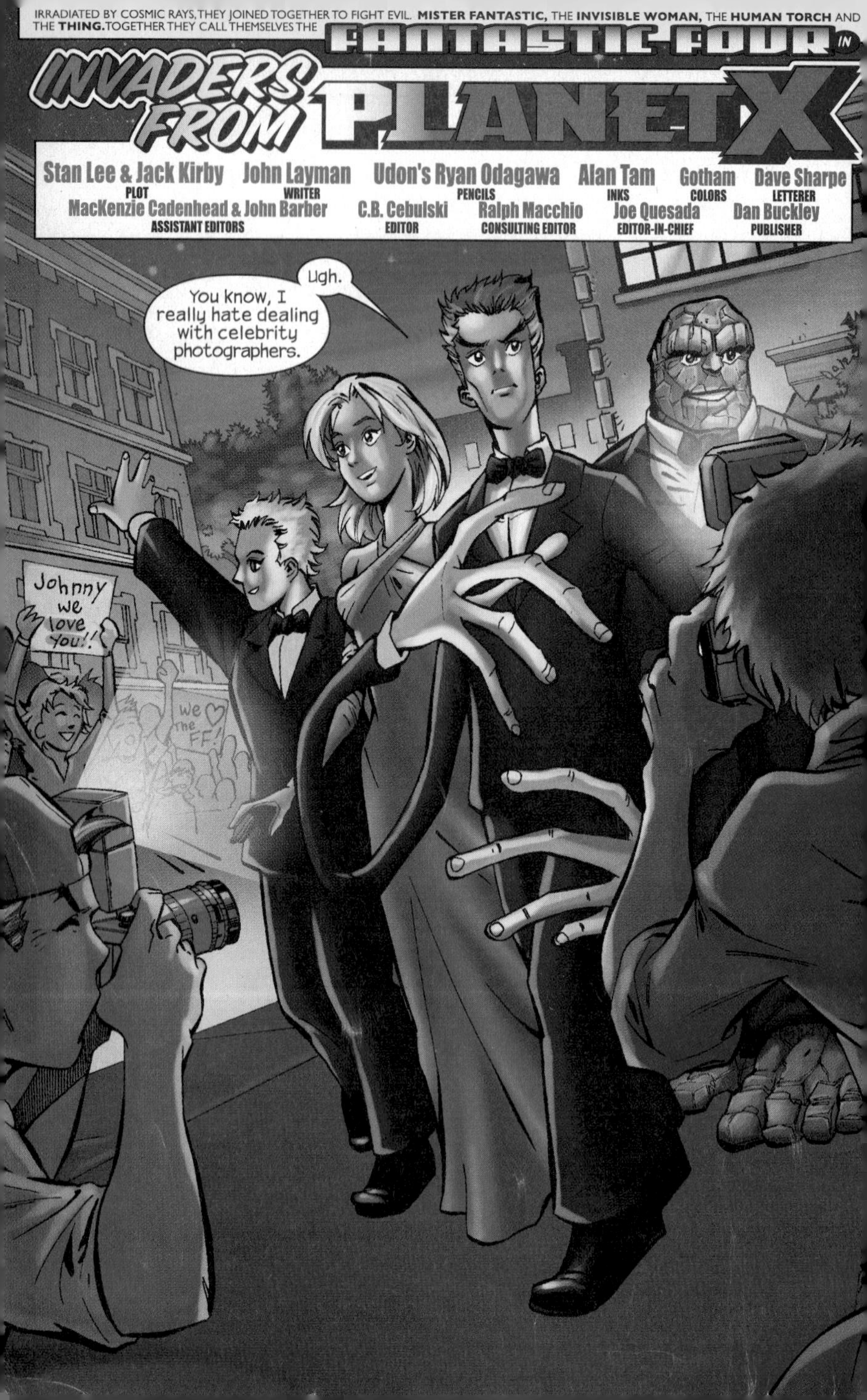

IRRADIATED BY COSMIC RAYS, THEY JOINED TOGETHER TO FIGHT EVIL. MISTER FANTASTIC, THE INVISIBLE WOMAN, THE HUMAN TORCH AND THE THING. TOGETHER THEY CALL THEMSELVES THE FANTASTIC FOUR IN
INVADERS FROM PLANET X
Stan Lee & Jack Kirby PLOT
John Layman WRITER
Udon's Ryan Odagawa PENCILS
Alan Tam INKS
Gotham COLORS
Dave Sharpe LETTERER
MacKenzie Cadenhead & John Barber ASSISTANT EDITORS
C.B. Cebulski EDITOR
Ralph Macchio CONSULTING EDITOR
Joe Quesada EDITOR-IN-CHIEF
Dan Buckley PUBLISHER
You know, I really hate dealing with celebrity photographers.
Ugh.
Johnny we love you!!
We ♡ the FF!

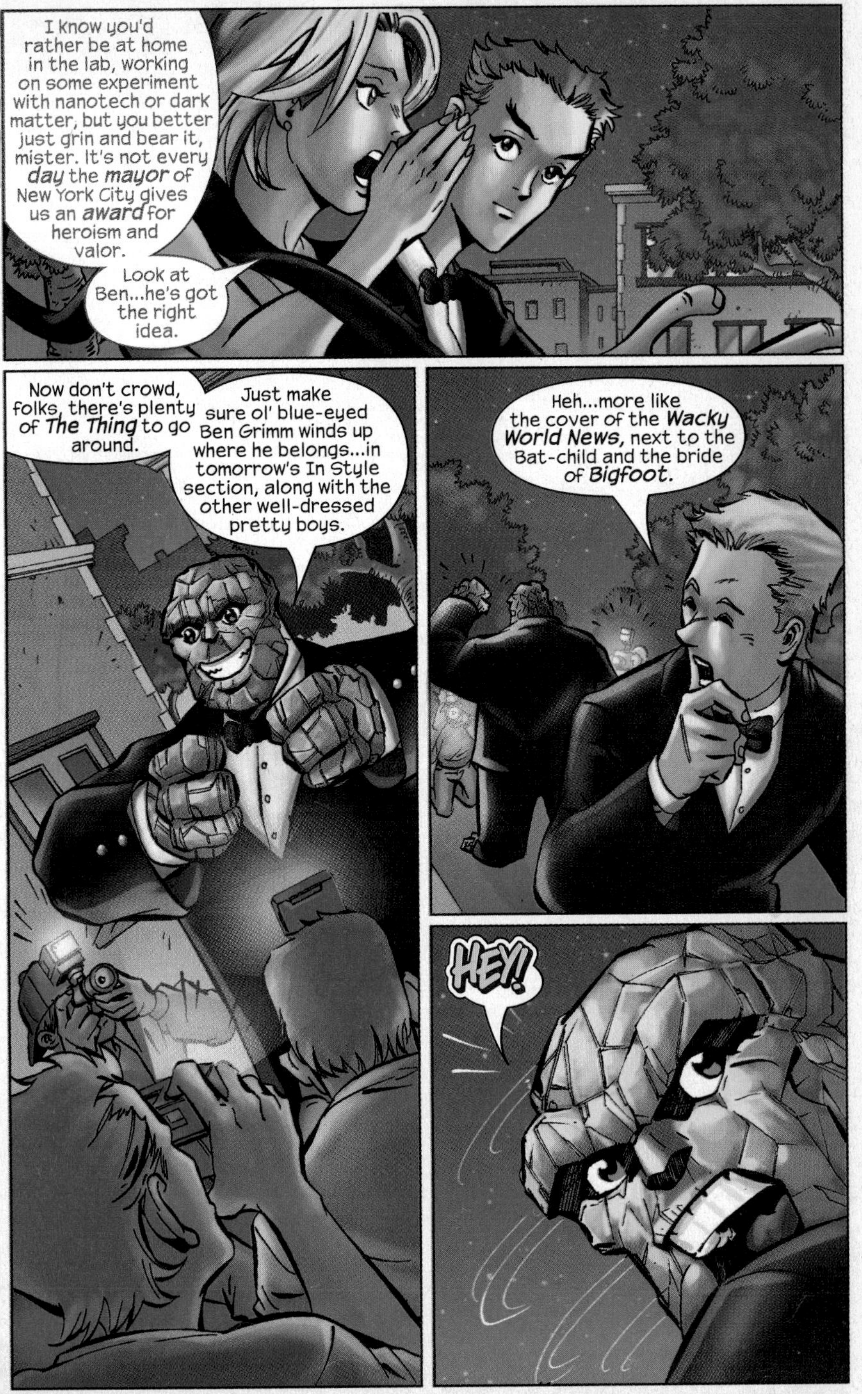

I know you'd rather be at home in the lab, working on some experiment with nanotech or dark matter, but you better just grin and bear it, mister. It's not every *day* the *mayor* of New York City gives us an *award* for heroism and valor.
Look at Ben...he's got the right idea.
Now don't crowd, folks, there's plenty of *The Thing* to go around.
Just make sure ol' blue-eyed Ben Grimm winds up where he belongs...in tomorrow's In Style section, along with the other well-dressed pretty boys.
Heh...more like the cover of the *Wacky World News*, next to the Bat-child and the bride of *Bigfoot*.
HEY!

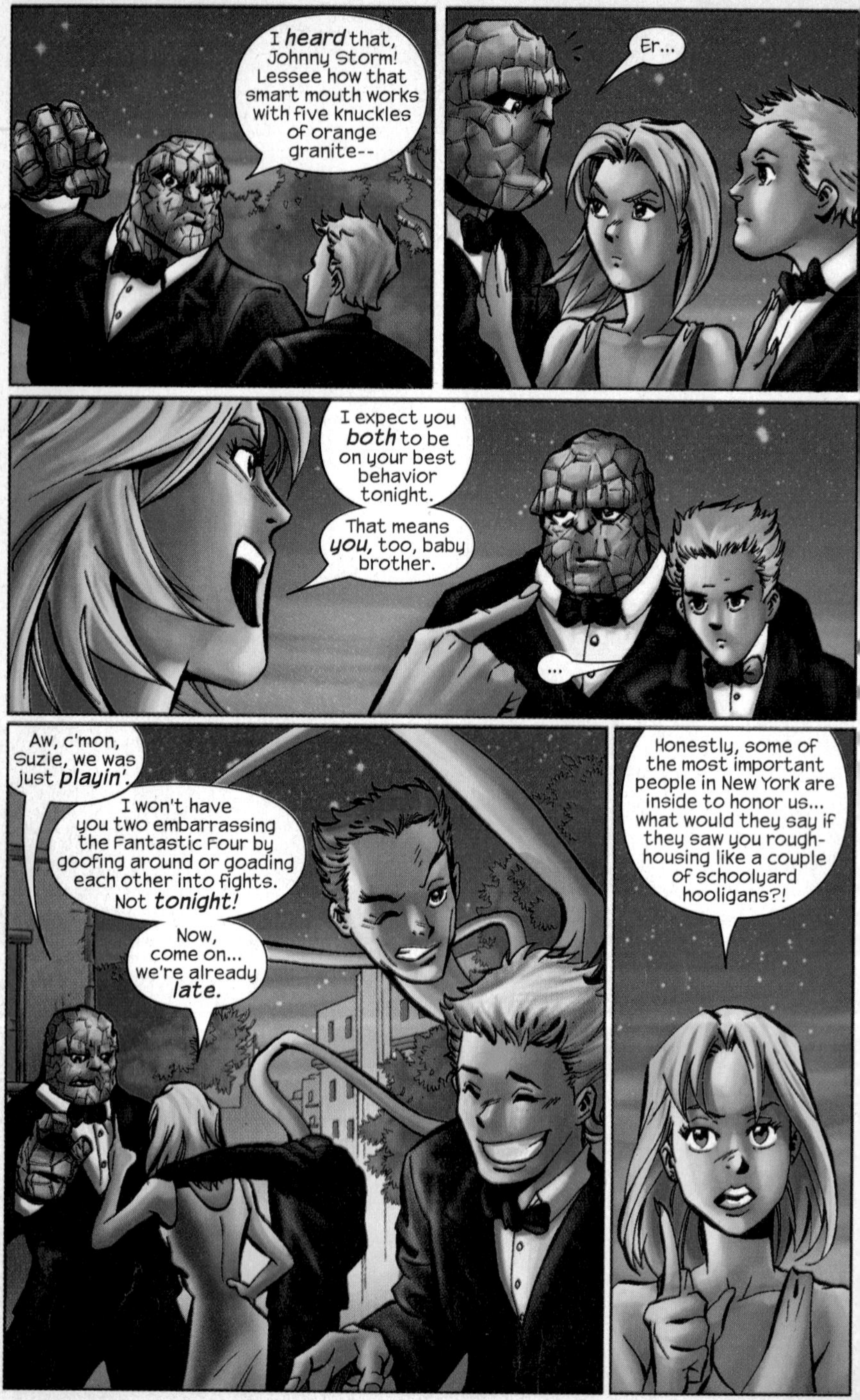
I heard that, Johnny Storm! Lessee how that smart mouth works with five knuckles of orange granite--
Er...
I expect you both to be on your best behavior tonight.
That means you, too, baby brother.
...
Aw, c'mon, Suzie, we was just playin'.
I won't have you two embarrassing the Fantastic Four by goofing around or goading each other into fights. Not tonight!
Now, come on... we're already late.
Honestly, some of the most important people in New York are inside to honor us... what would they say if they saw you rough-housing like a couple of schoolyard hooligans?!

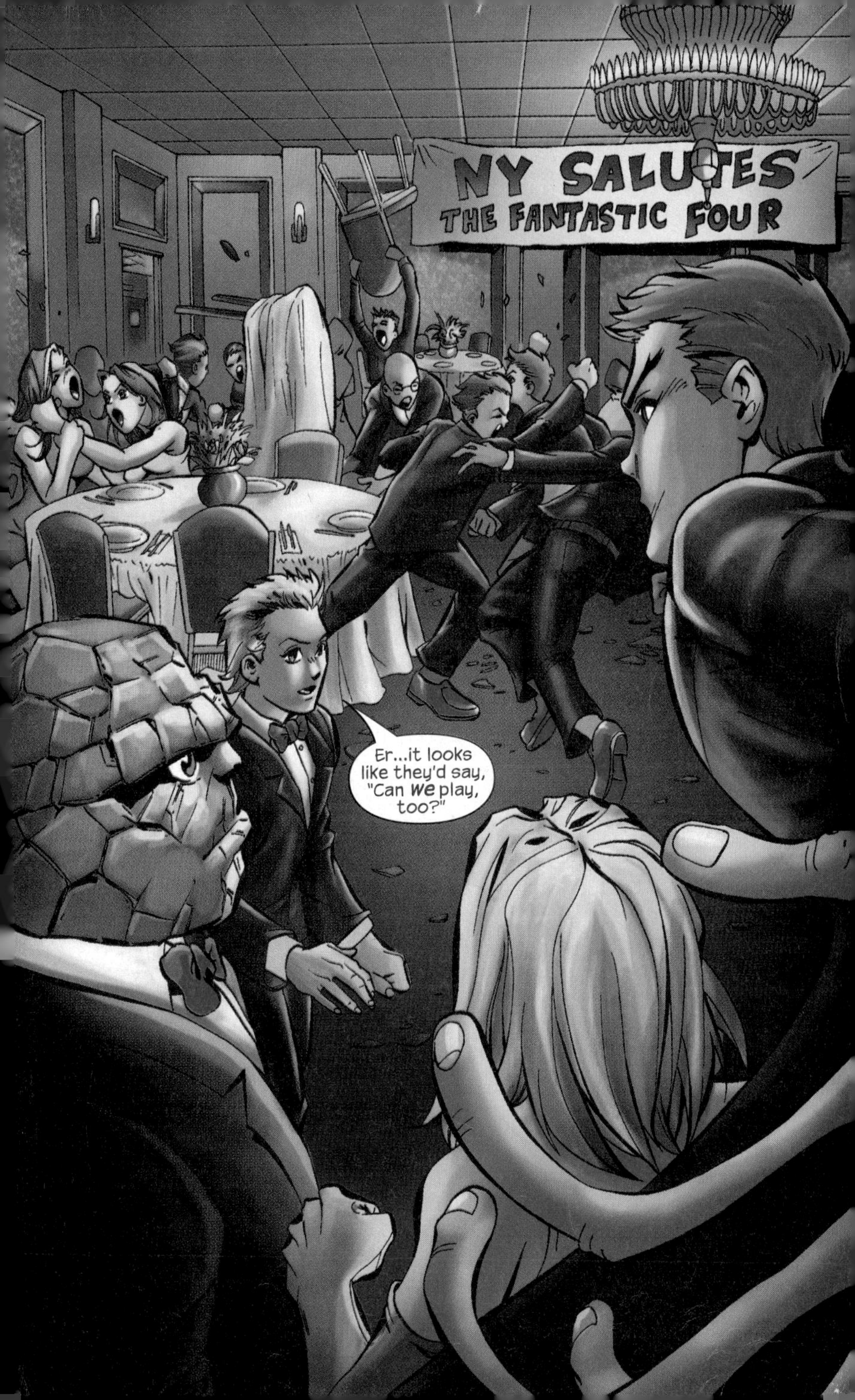
NY SALUTES THE FANTASTIC FOUR
Er...it looks like they'd say, "Can *we* play, too?"

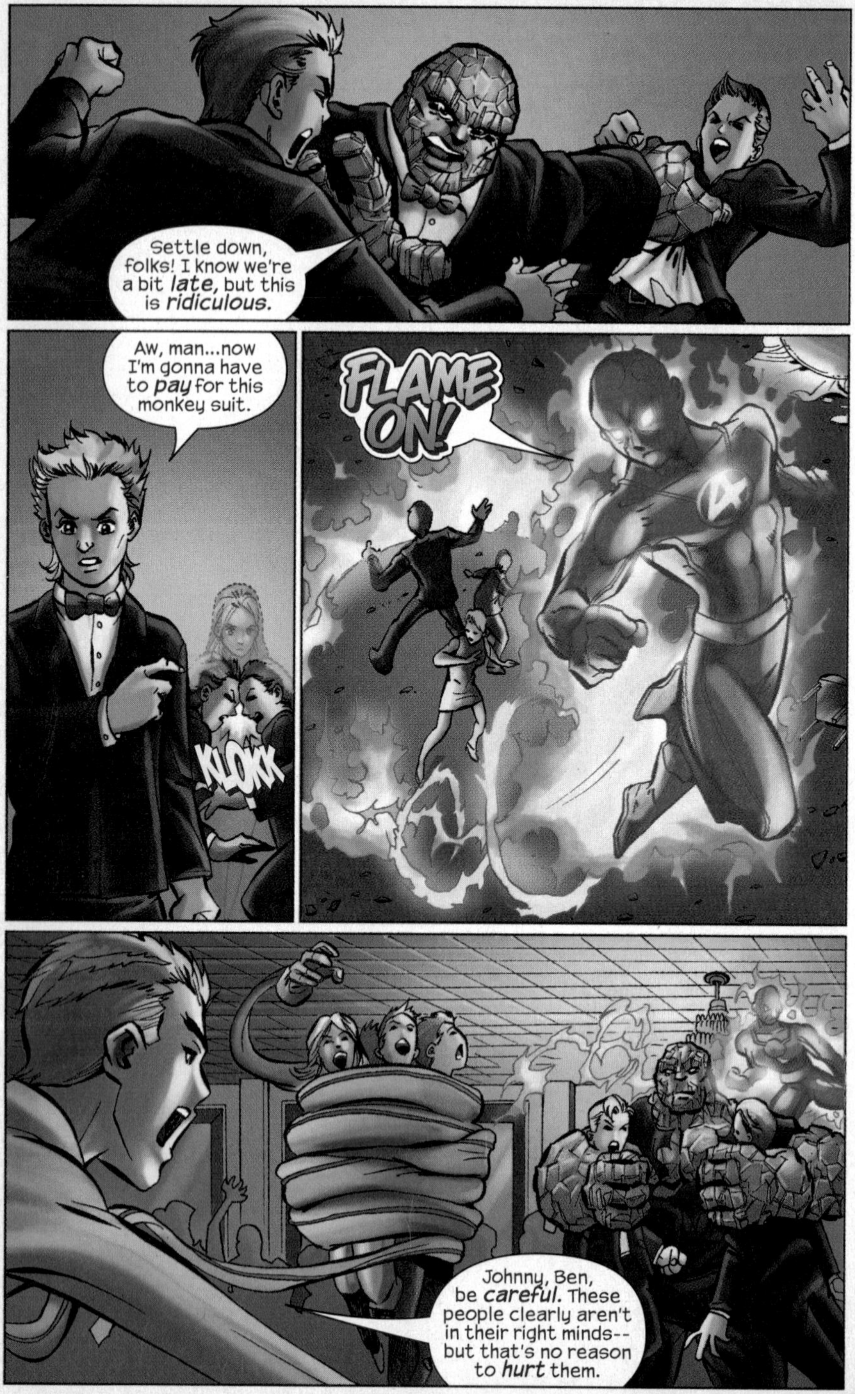
Settle down, folks! I know we're a bit late, but this is ridiculous.
Aw, man...now I'm gonna have to pay for this monkey suit.
KLOKK
FLAME ON!
Johnny, Ben, be careful. These people clearly aren't in their right minds-- but that's no reason to hurt them.

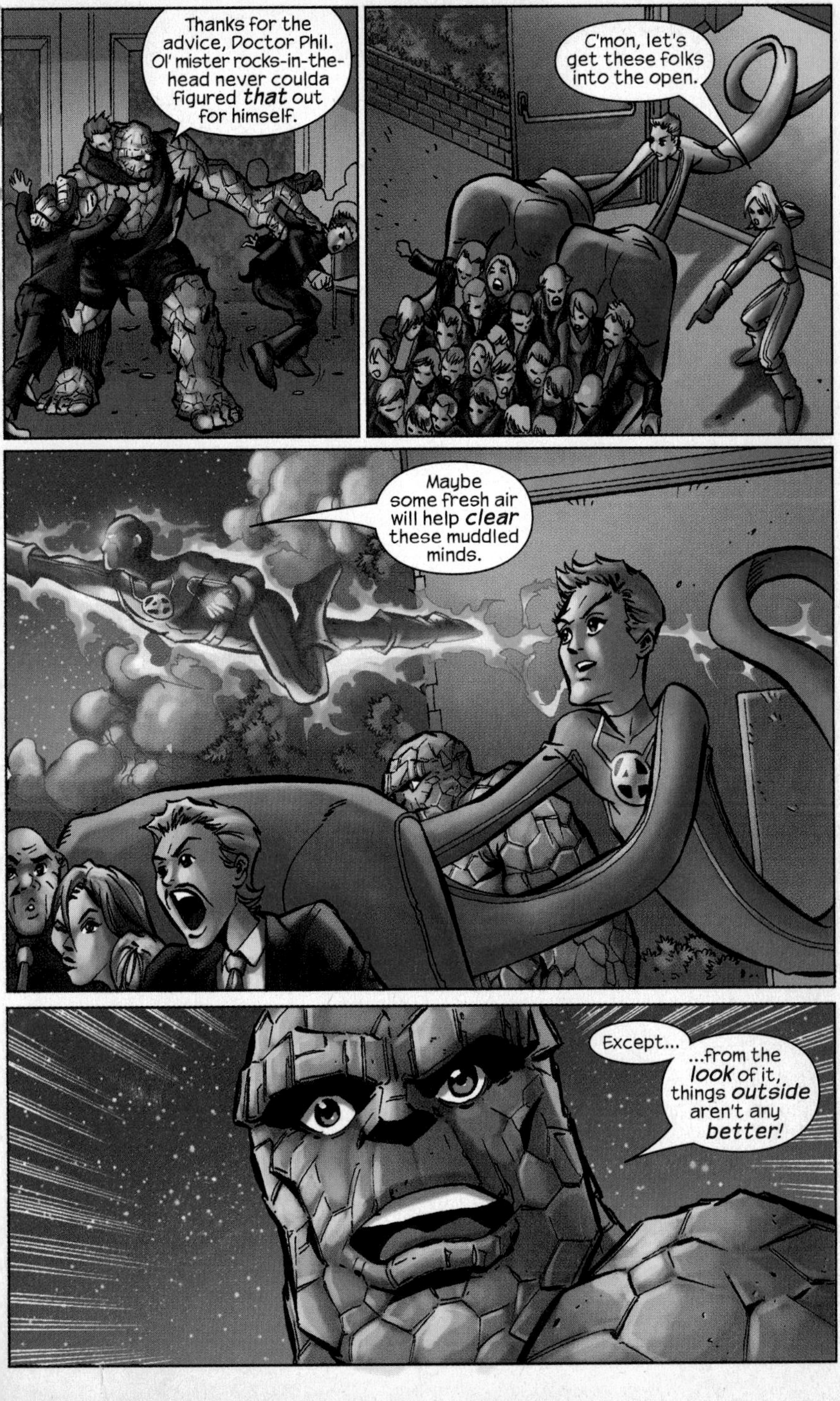
Thanks for the advice, Doctor Phil. Ol' mister rocks-in-the-head never coulda figured *that* out for himself.
C'mon, let's get these folks into the open.
Maybe some fresh air will help *clear* these muddled minds.
Except...
...from the *look* of it, things *outside* aren't any *better!*

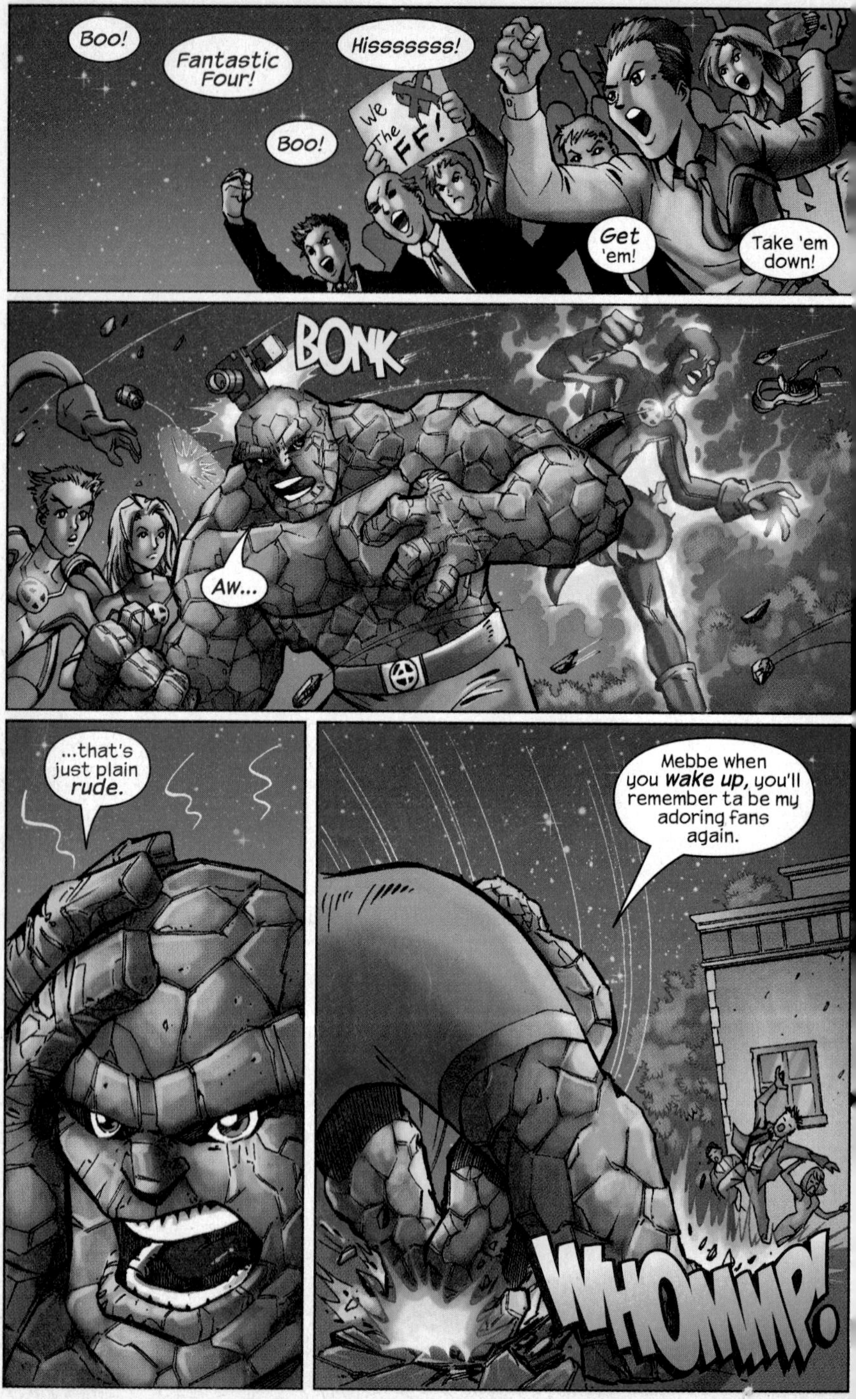
Boo!
Fantastic Four!
Hisssssss!
Boo!
We [X] The FF!
Get 'em!
Take 'em down!
BONK
Aw...
...that's just plain *rude.*
Mebbe when you *wake up,* you'll remember ta be my adoring fans again.
WHOMMP!

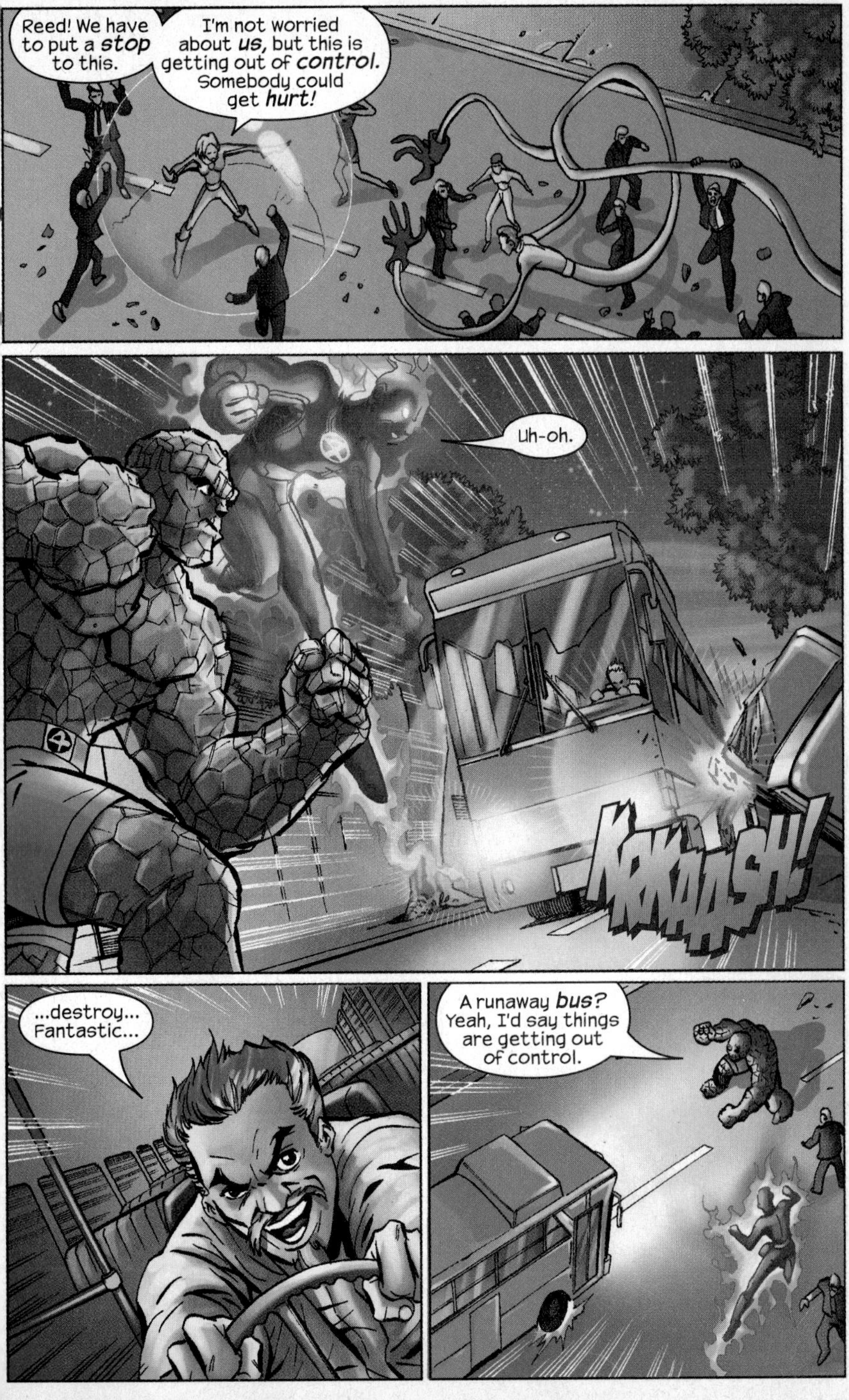
Reed! We have to put a stop to this.
I'm not worried about us, but this is getting out of control. Somebody could get hurt!
Uh-oh.
KRAASH!
...destroy... Fantastic...
A runaway bus? Yeah, I'd say things are getting out of control.

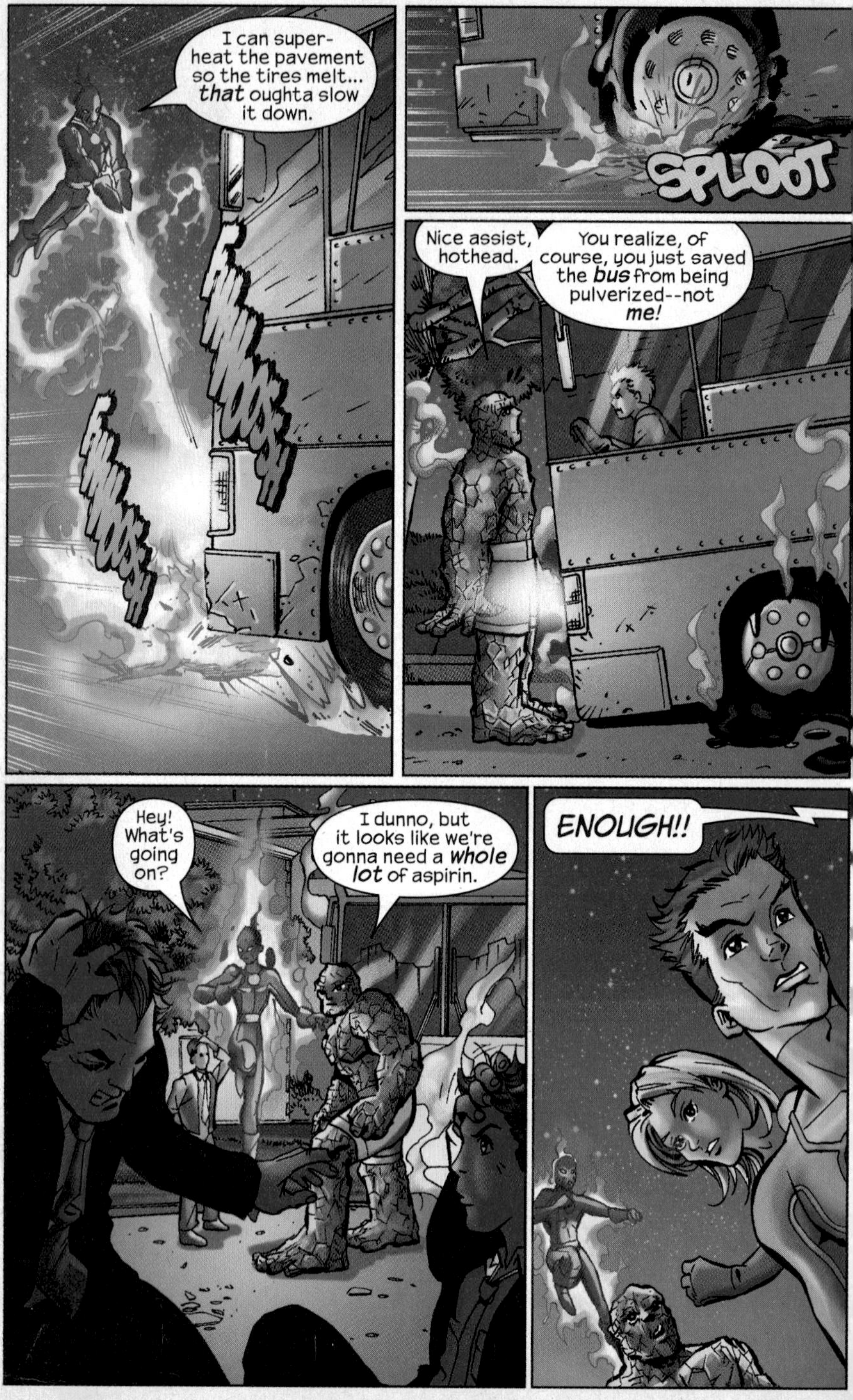
I can super-heat the pavement so the tires melt... *that* oughta slow it down.
FWOOSH
FWOOSH
SPLOOT
Nice assist, hothead.
You realize, of course, you just saved the *bus* from being pulverized--not *me!*
Hey! What's going on?
I dunno, but it looks like we're gonna need a *whole lot* of aspirin.
ENOUGH!!

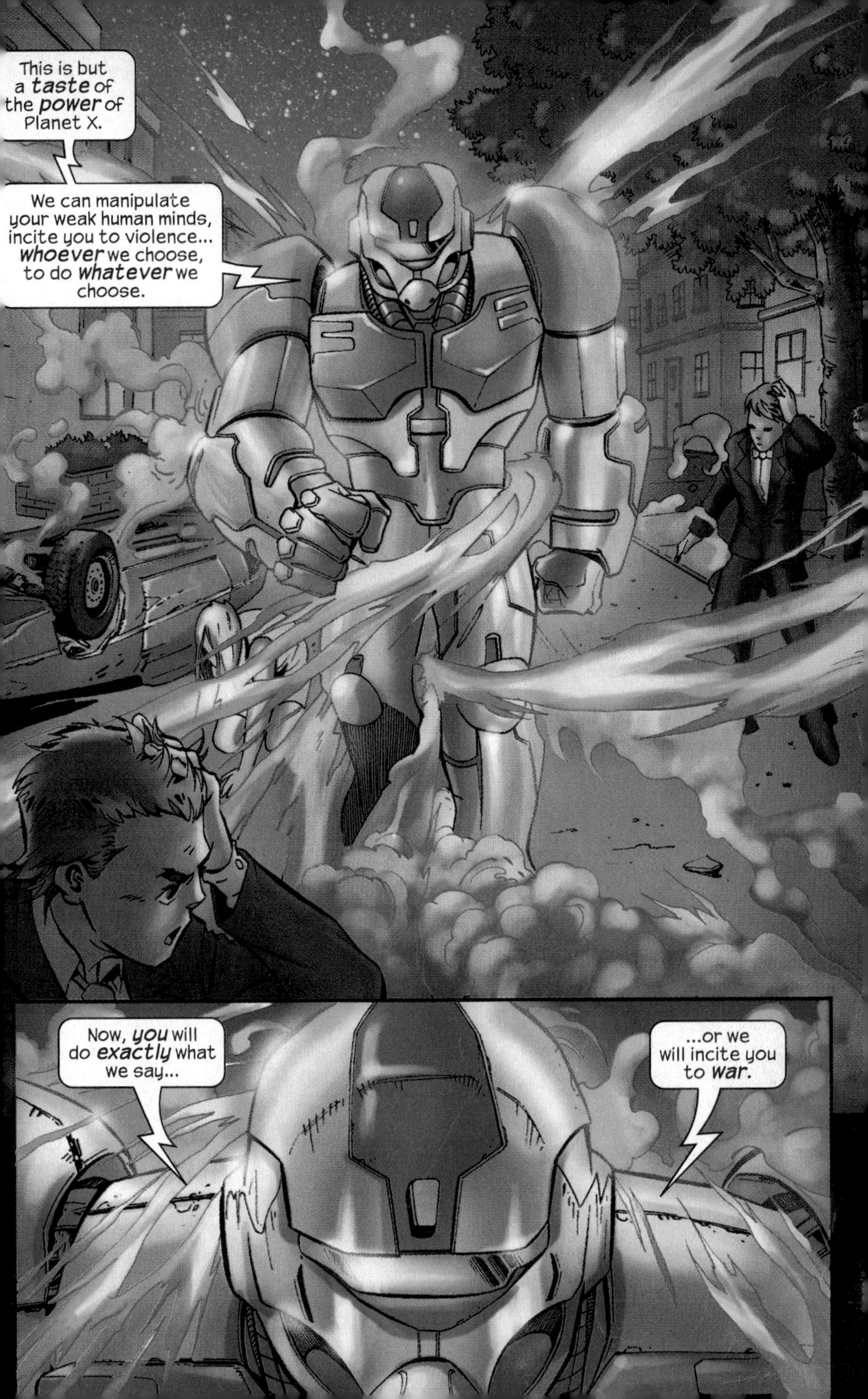
This is but a *taste* of the *power* of Planet X.
We can manipulate your weak human minds, incite you to violence... *whoever* we choose, to do *whatever* we choose.
Now, *you* will do *exactly* what we say...
...or we will incite you to *war*.

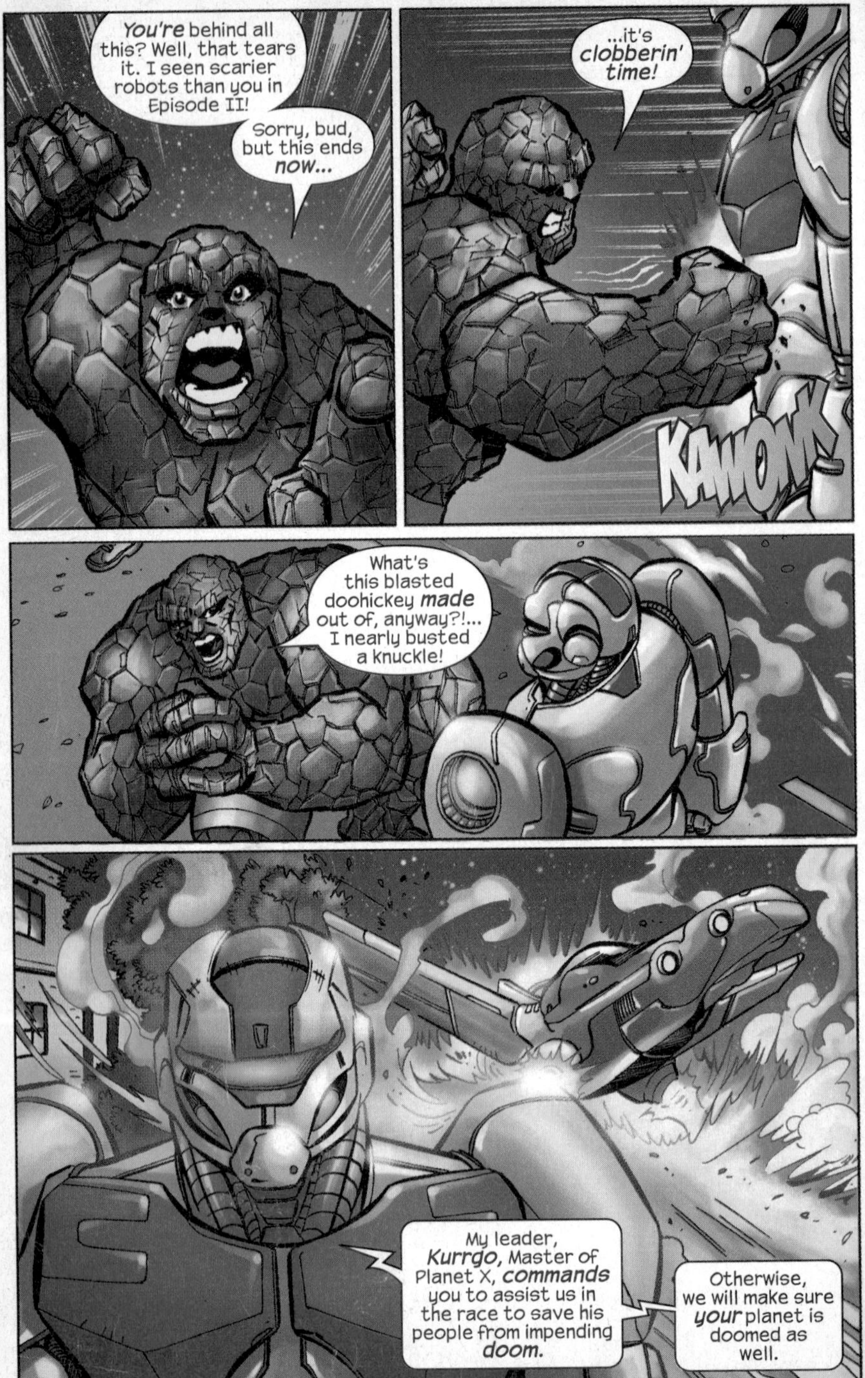
You're behind all this? Well, that tears it. I seen scarier robots than you in Episode II!
Sorry, bud, but this ends now...
...it's clobberin' time!
KAWONK
What's this blasted doohickey made out of, anyway?!... I nearly busted a knuckle!
My leader, Kurrgo, Master of Planet X, commands you to assist us in the race to save his people from impending doom.
Otherwise, we will make sure your planet is doomed as well.

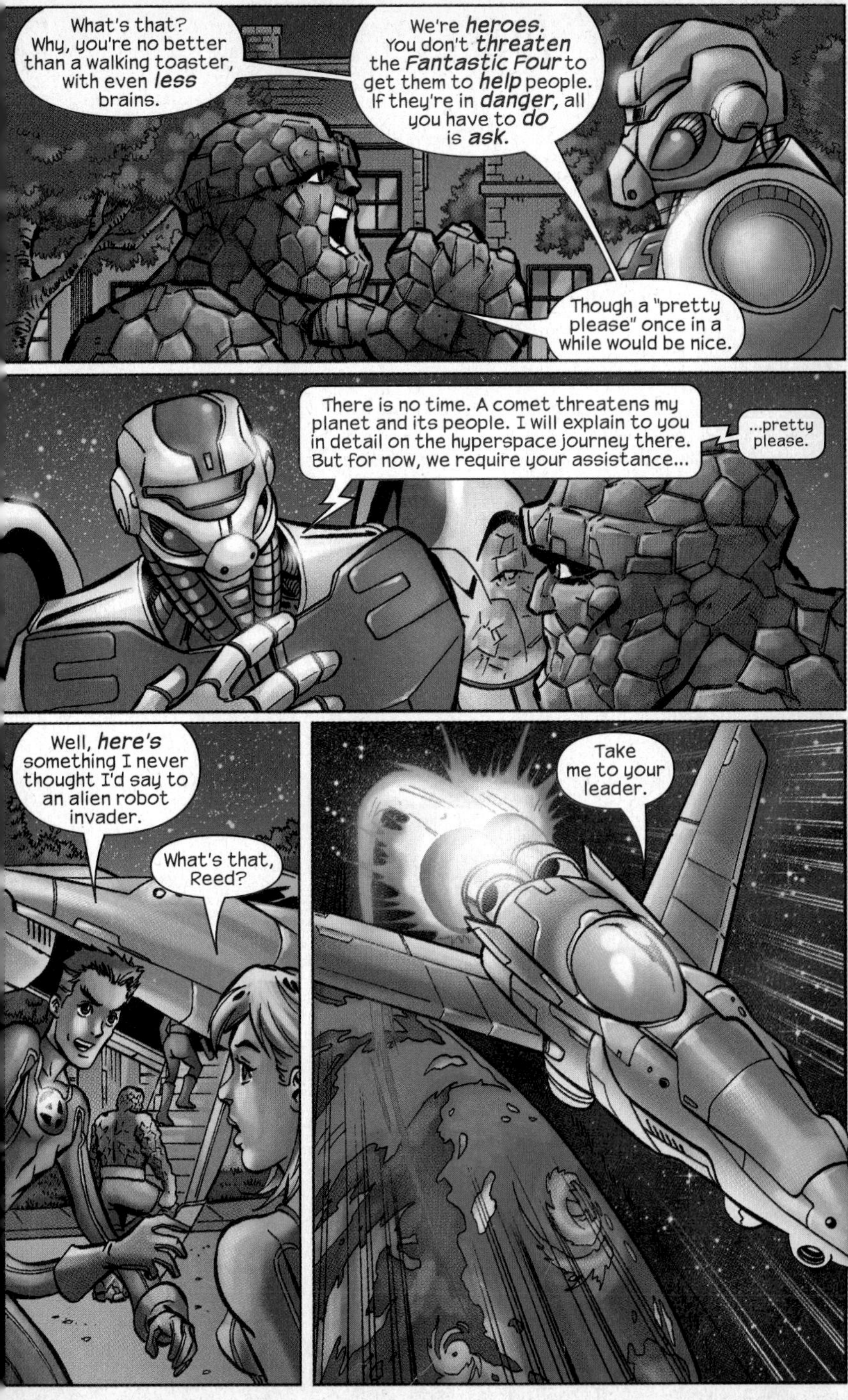
What's that? Why, you're no better than a walking toaster, with even *less* brains.
We're *heroes.* You don't *threaten* the *Fantastic Four* to get them to *help* people. If they're in *danger,* all you have to *do* is *ask.*
Though a "pretty please" once in a while would be nice.
There is no time. A comet threatens my planet and its people. I will explain to you in detail on the hyperspace journey there. But for now, we require your assistance...
...pretty please.
Well, *here's* something I never thought I'd say to an alien robot invader.
What's that, Reed?
Take me to your leader.

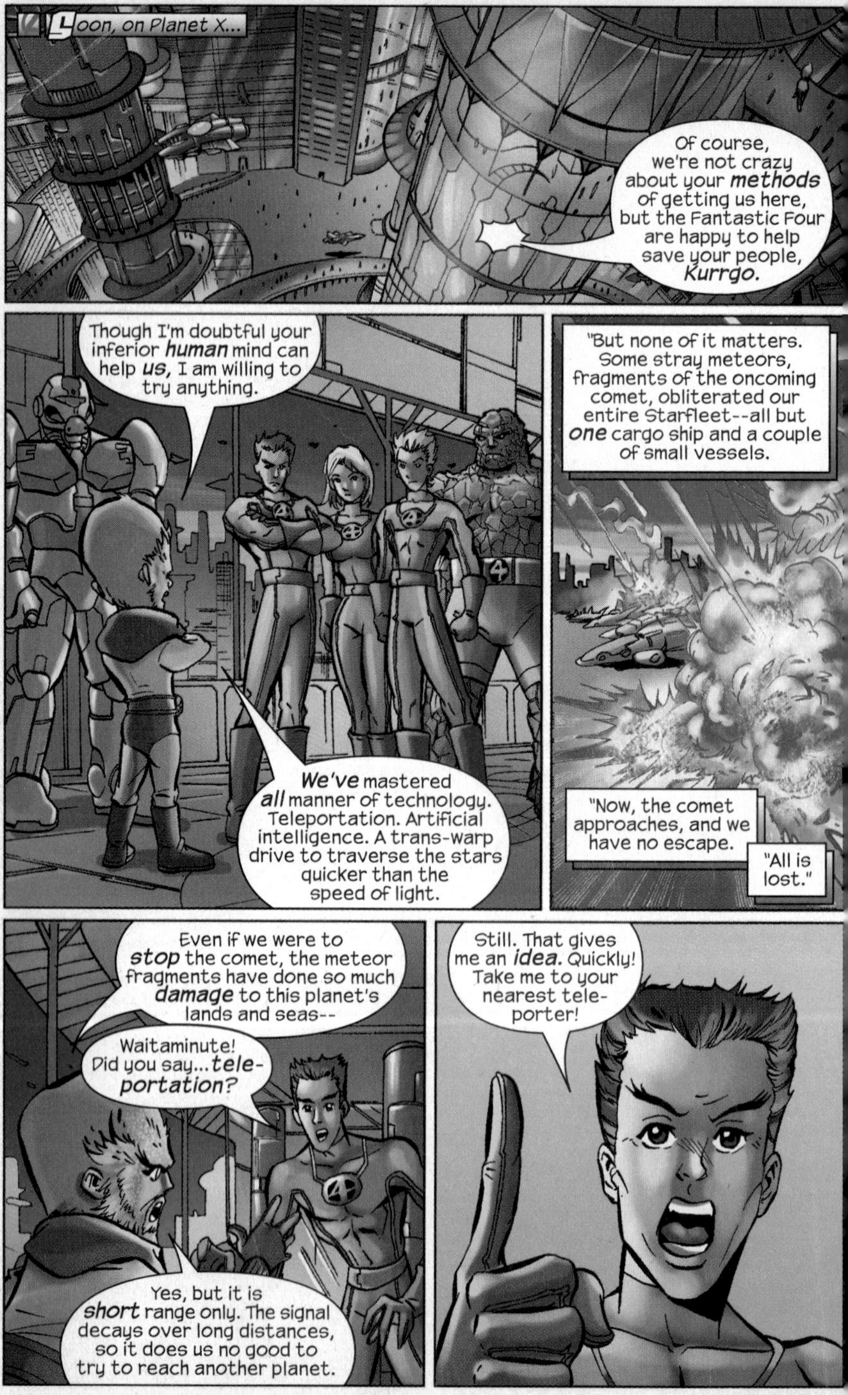
Soon, on Planet X...
Of course, we're not crazy about your methods of getting us here, but the Fantastic Four are happy to help save your people, Kurrgo.
Though I'm doubtful your inferior human mind can help us, I am willing to try anything.
We've mastered all manner of technology. Teleportation. Artificial intelligence. A trans-warp drive to traverse the stars quicker than the speed of light.
"But none of it matters. Some stray meteors, fragments of the oncoming comet, obliterated our entire Starfleet--all but one cargo ship and a couple of small vessels.
"Now, the comet approaches, and we have no escape.
"All is lost."
Even if we were to stop the comet, the meteor fragments have done so much damage to this planet's lands and seas--
Waitaminute! Did you say...tele-portation?
Yes, but it is short range only. The signal decays over long distances, so it does us no good to try to reach another planet.
Still. That gives me an idea. Quickly! Take me to your nearest tele-porter!

Hmm...so what do you figure ol' Big Brain is up to in there?

I dunno. Maybe trying to figure out a way to make their teleportation technology *long-range?*

Good guess, Johnny, but not quite.

"You see, as I suspected, the technology Kurrgo's people have for teleportation catalogs and breaks down matter at an atomic level, then sends the information to a teleport-receiver in particle waves."

"Encoded information from one place to the next? Kinda like an e-mail?"

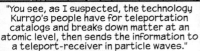

Well, not exactly, though you're not *too* far off. You see, there is *so* much information because there are so many *atoms* to catalog, disassemble and reconstruct.

Some of it is bound to get lost in transition. The only way to ensure this does not happen is to send things over a very short distance.

≥yawn≤

So, uh, how 'bout the short version, stretch pants? You built a *booster*, right?

The "*short*" version, eh? Follow me.

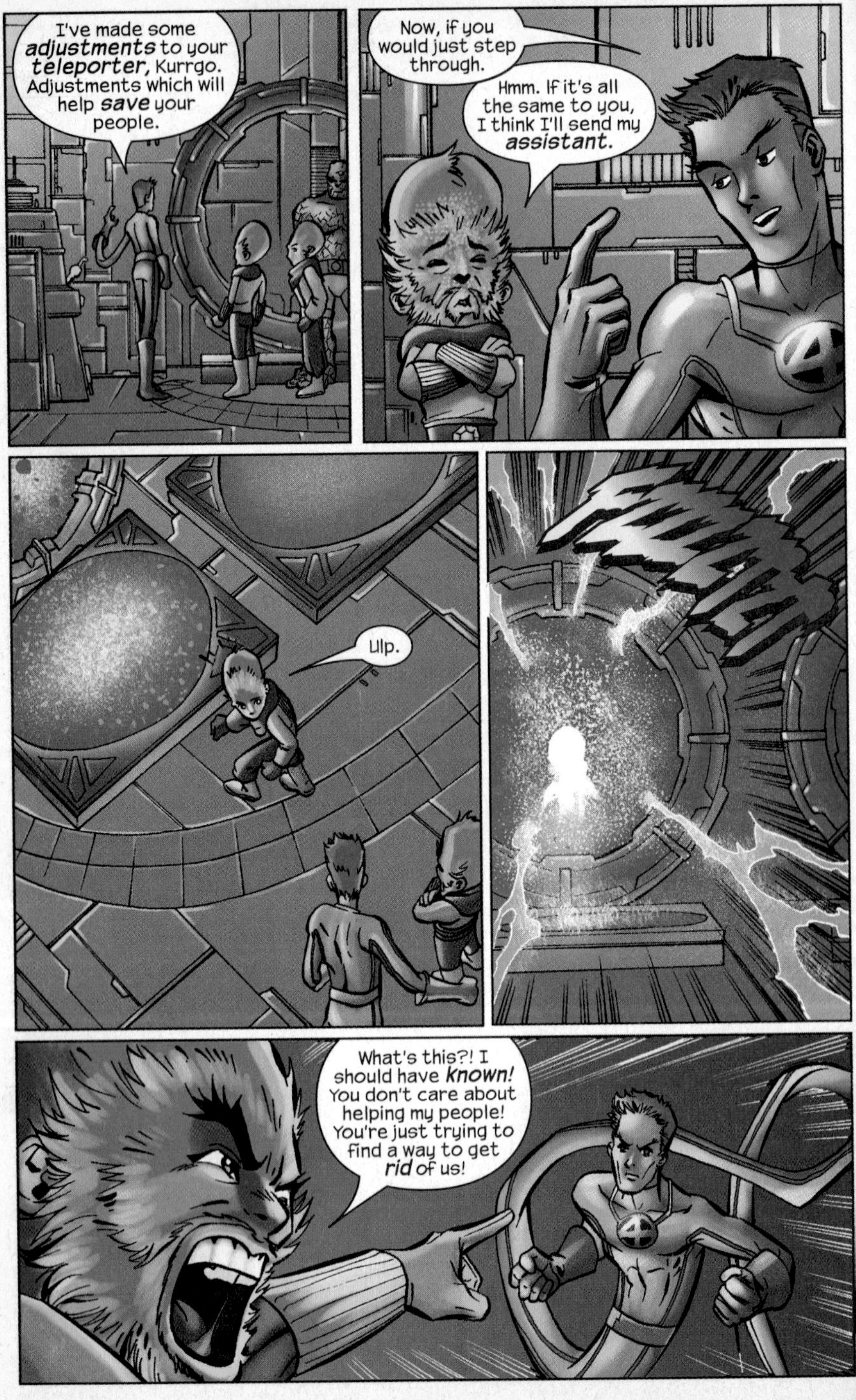
I've made some adjustments to your teleporter, Kurrgo. Adjustments which will help save your people.
Now, if you would just step through.
Hmm. If it's all the same to you, I think I'll send my assistant.
Ulp.
What's this?! I should have known! You don't care about helping my people! You're just trying to find a way to get rid of us!

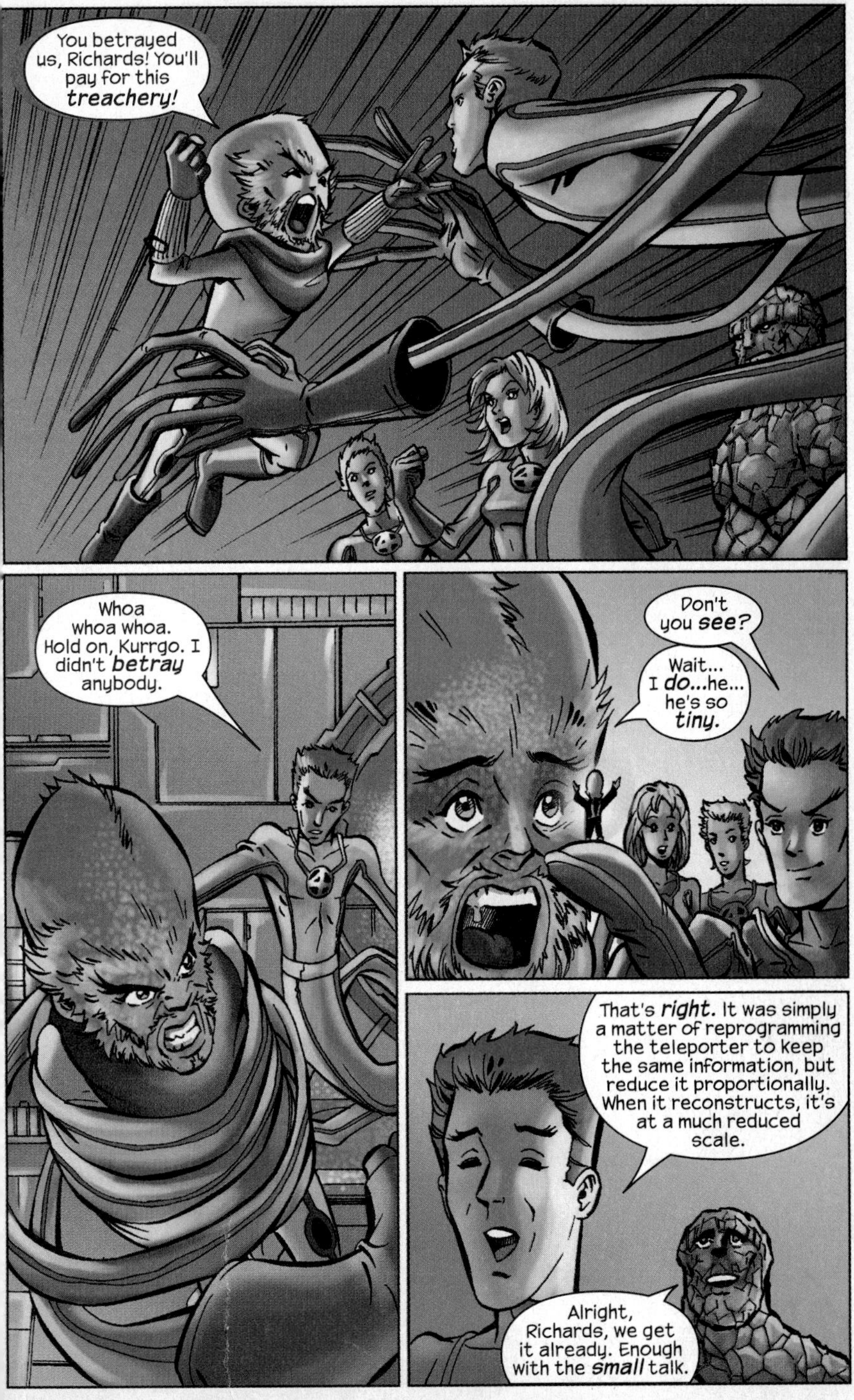

You betrayed us, Richards! You'll pay for this *treachery!*
Whoa whoa whoa. Hold on, Kurrgo. I didn't *betray* anybody.
Don't you *see?*
Wait... I *do*...he... he's so *tiny.*
That's *right.* It was simply a matter of reprogramming the teleporter to keep the same information, but reduce it proportionally. When it reconstructs, it's at a much reduced scale.
Alright, Richards, we get it already. Enough with the *small* talk.

Shrinking us may be the best way to make us less of a *threat*, but I fail to see how that *saves* us.

Man, for an advanced civilization, you're pretty darned *thick*. Doncha *get* it, Kurrgo? *Now* there will be *room* for *all* of you on that last cargo ship.

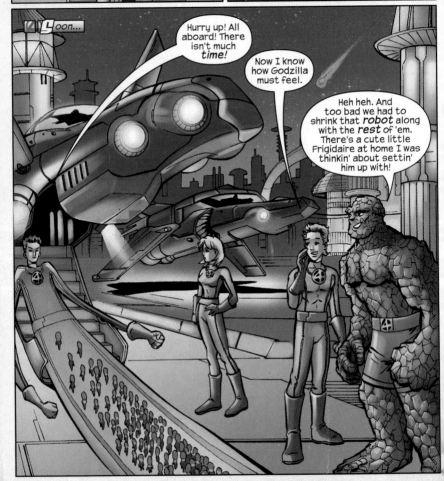

Soon...

Hurry up! All aboard! There isn't much *time!*

Now I know how Godzilla must feel.

Heh heh. And too bad we had to shrink that *robot* along with the *rest* of 'em. There's a cute little Frigidaire at home I was thinkin' about settin' him up with!

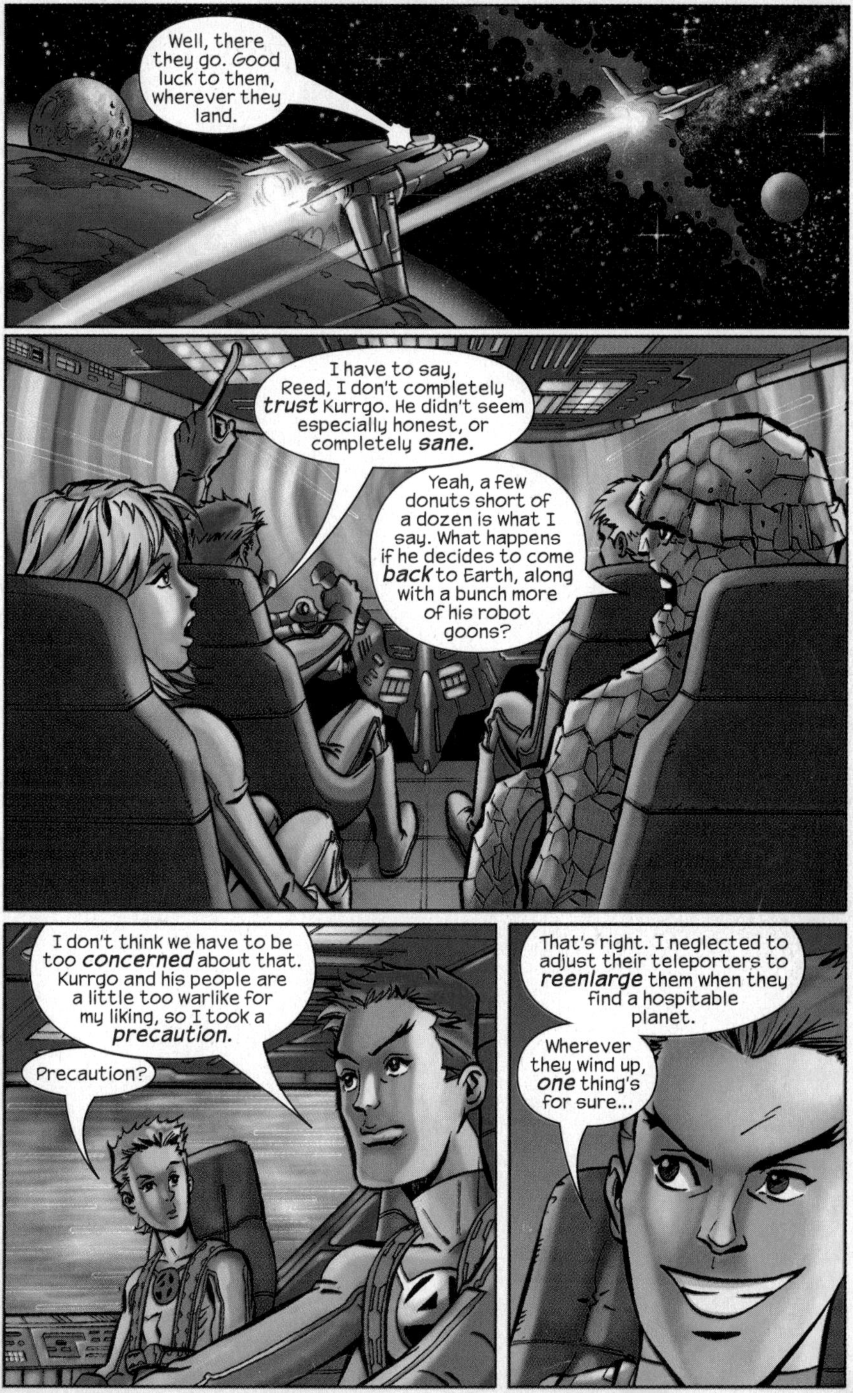
Well, there they go. Good luck to them, wherever they land.
I have to say, Reed, I don't completely *trust* Kurrgo. He didn't seem especially honest, or completely *sane.*
Yeah, a few donuts short of a dozen is what I say. What happens if he decides to come *back* to Earth, along with a bunch more of his robot goons?
I don't think we have to be too *concerned* about that. Kurrgo and his people are a little too warlike for my liking, so I took a *precaution.*
Precaution?
That's right. I neglected to adjust their teleporters to *reenlarge* them when they find a hospitable planet.
Wherever they wind up, *one* thing's for sure...

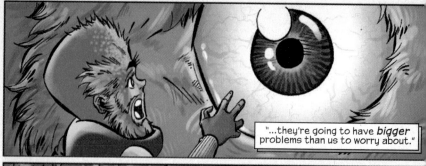

"...they're going to have *bigger* problems than us to worry about."

Hahahah. Quick thinking, Reed.

Yeah, good job, Stretcho. Now ya *think* you can get this bucket of bolts to move any faster? I'm missin' a new episode of "Survivor."

The end.

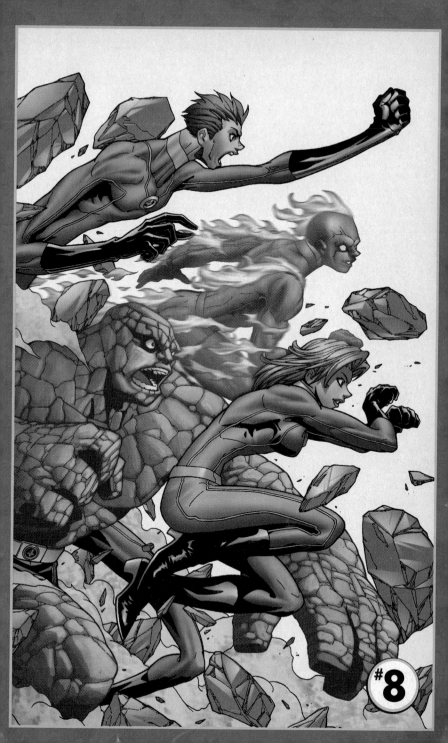

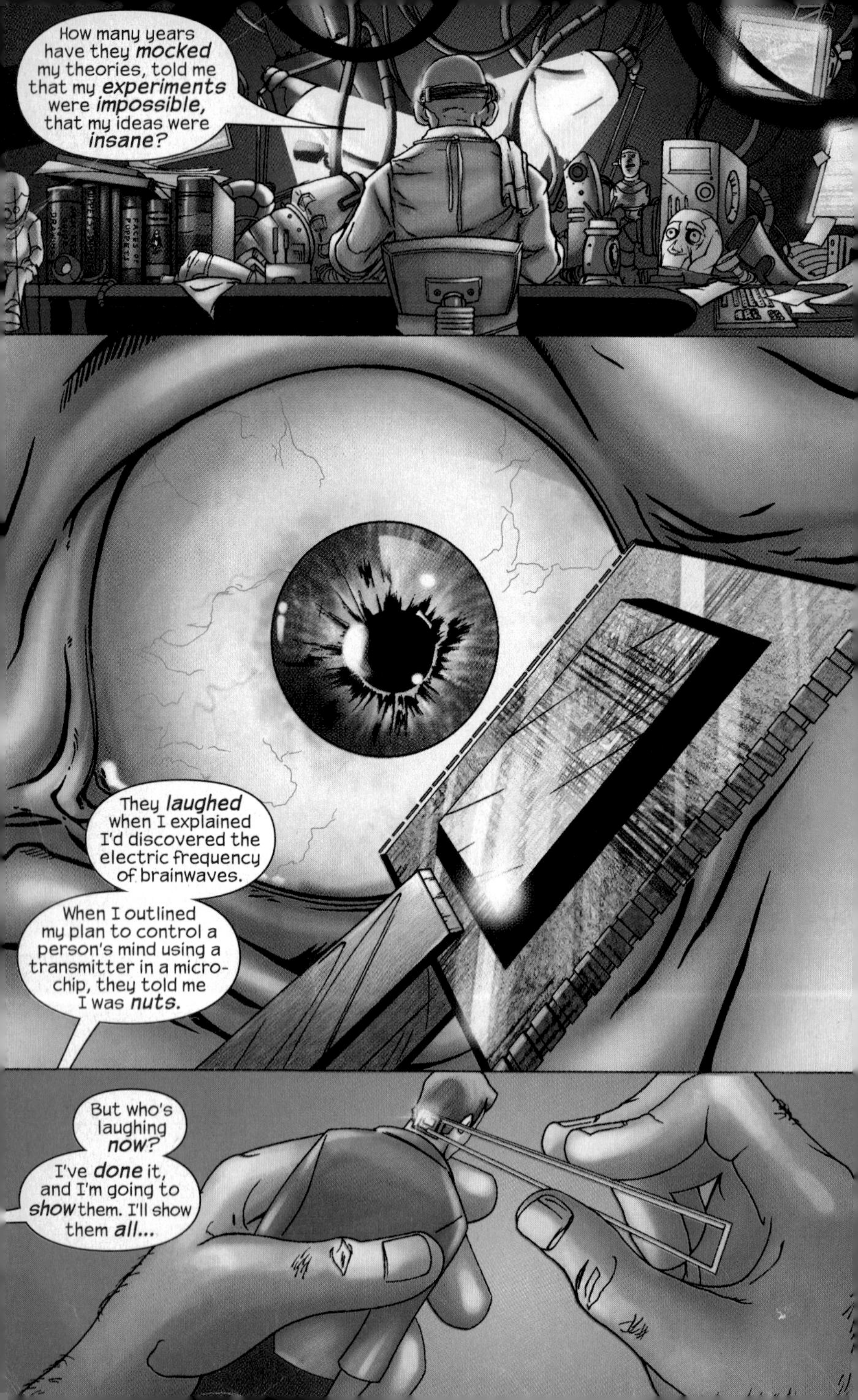
How many years have they mocked my theories, told me that my experiments were impossible, that my ideas were insane?
They laughed when I explained I'd discovered the electric frequency of brainwaves.
When I outlined my plan to control a person's mind using a transmitter in a micro-chip, they told me I was nuts.
But who's laughing now?
I've done it, and I'm going to show them. I'll show them all...

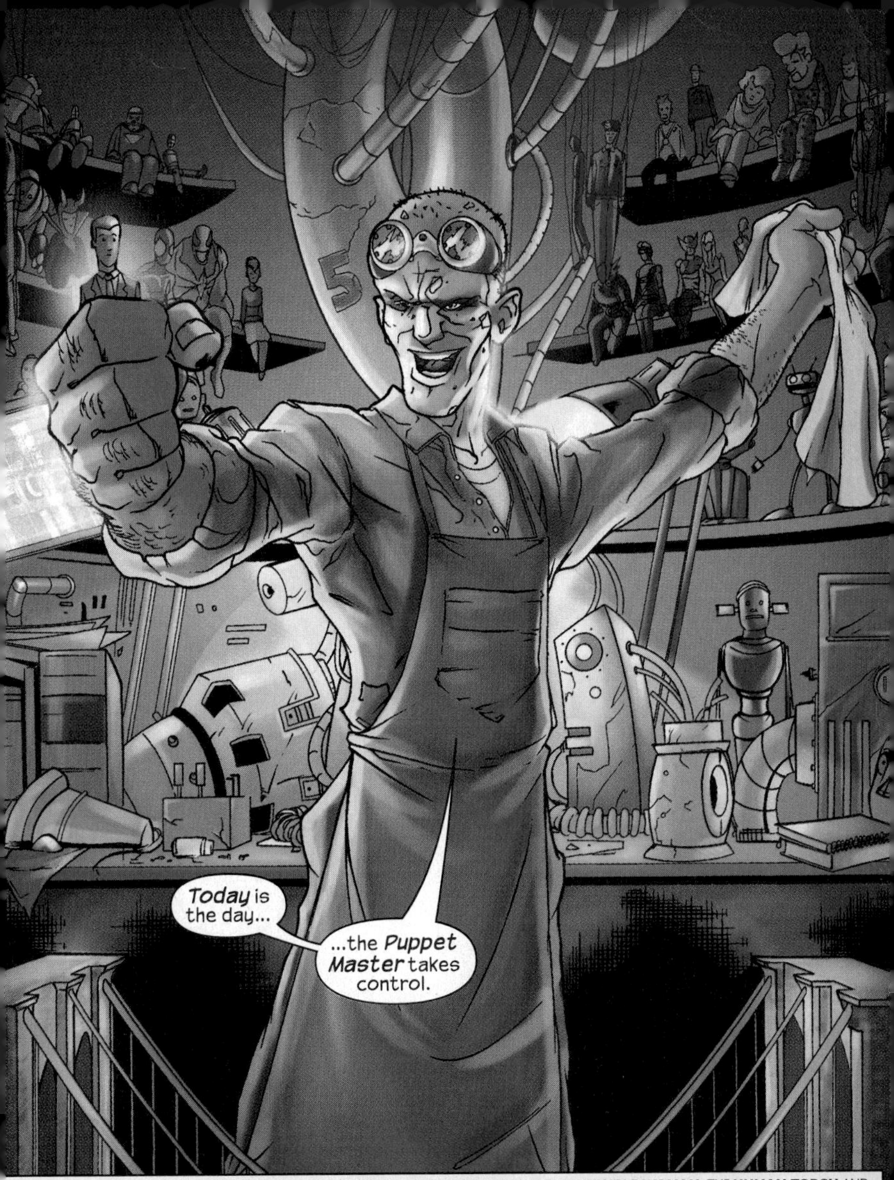
Today is the day...
...the Puppet Master takes control.

IRRADIATED BY COSMIC RAYS, THEY JOINED TOGETHER TO FIGHT EVIL. **MISTER FANTASTIC,** THE **INVISIBLE WOMAN,** THE **HUMAN TORCH** AND THE **THING.** TOGETHER THEY CALL THEMSELVES THE **FANTASTIC FOUR** IN

Prisoners of the Puppet Master!

Stan Lee & Jack Kirby PLOT
John Layman WRITER
Joseph Dodd PENCILS
Justin Holman INKS
Gotham COLORS
Dave Sharpe LETTERER
MacKenzie Cadenhead & John Barber ASSISTANT EDITORS
C.B. Cebulski EDITOR
Ralph Macchio CONSULTING EDITOR
Joe Quesada EDITOR-IN-CHIEF
Dan Buckley PUBLISHER

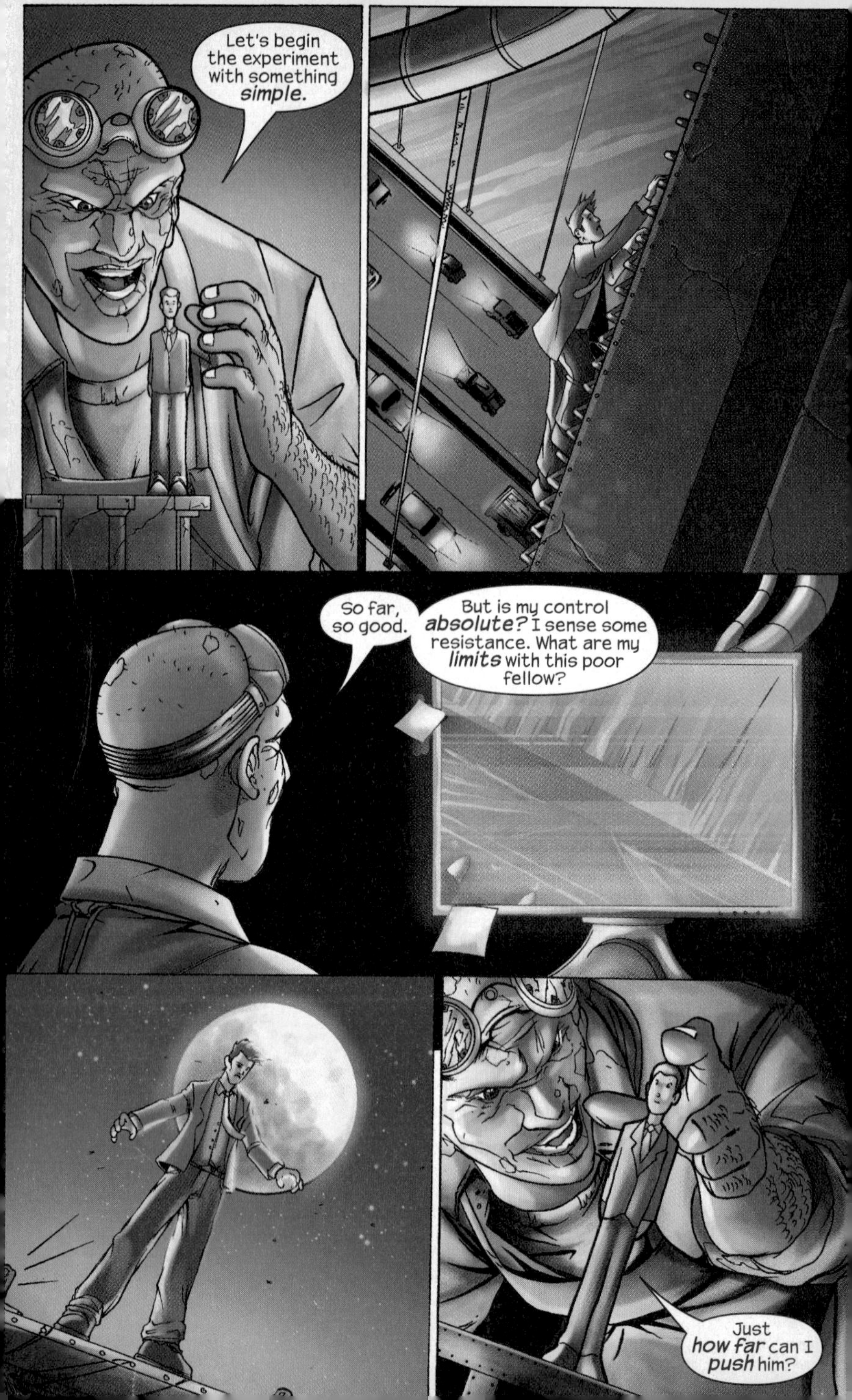
Let's begin the experiment with something *simple.*
So far, so good.
But is my control *absolute?* I sense some resistance. What are my *limits* with this poor fellow?
Just *how far* can I *push* him?

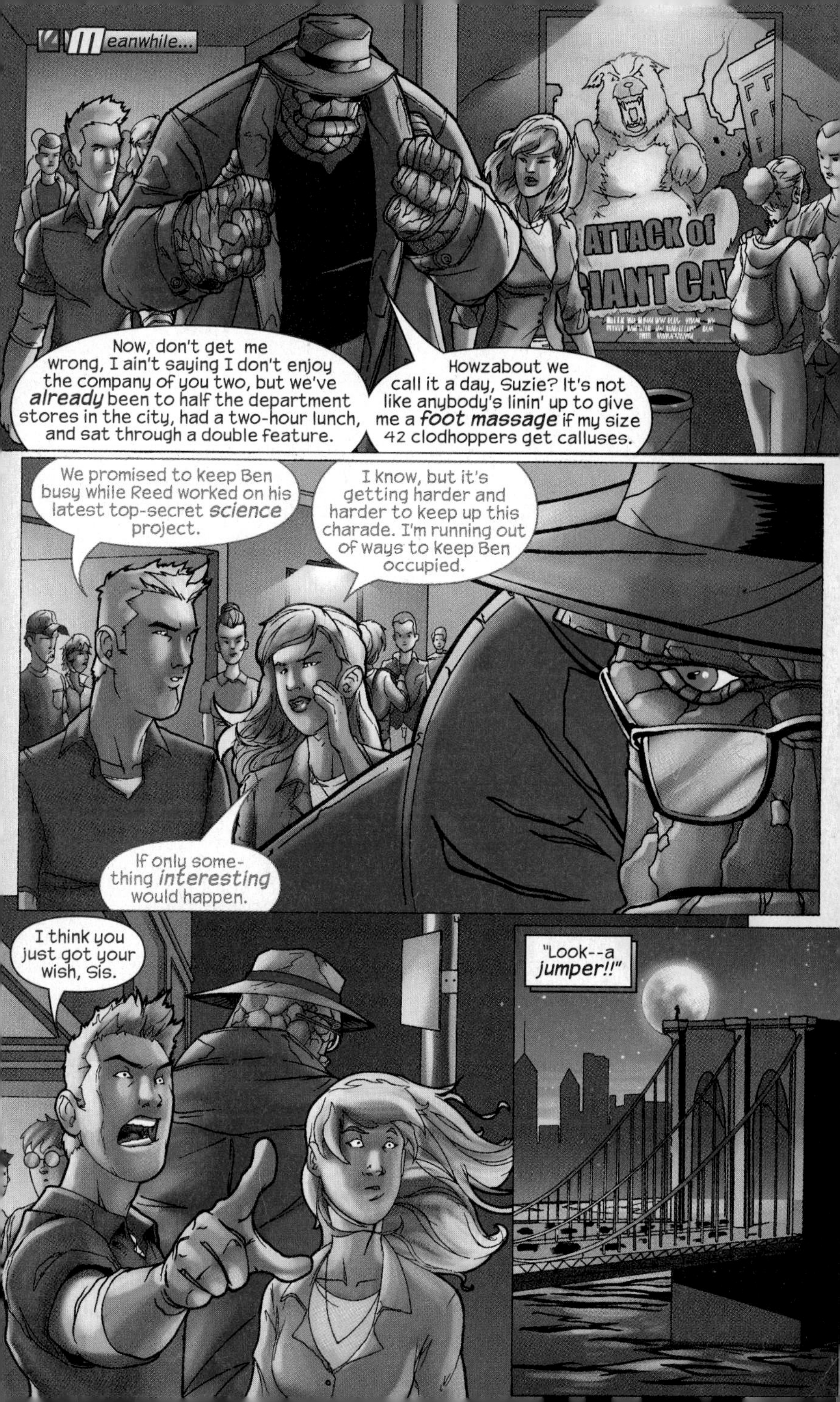
Meanwhile...
Now, don't get me wrong, I ain't saying I don't enjoy the company of you two, but we've *already* been to half the department stores in the city, had a two-hour lunch, and sat through a double feature.
Howzabout we call it a day, Suzie? It's not like anybody's linin' up to give me a *foot massage* if my size 42 clodhoppers get calluses.
ATTACK of GIANT CAT
We promised to keep Ben busy while Reed worked on his latest top-secret *science* project.
I know, but it's getting harder and harder to keep up this charade. I'm running out of ways to keep Ben occupied.
If only something *interesting* would happen.
I think you just got your wish, Sis.
"Look--a *jumper!!*"

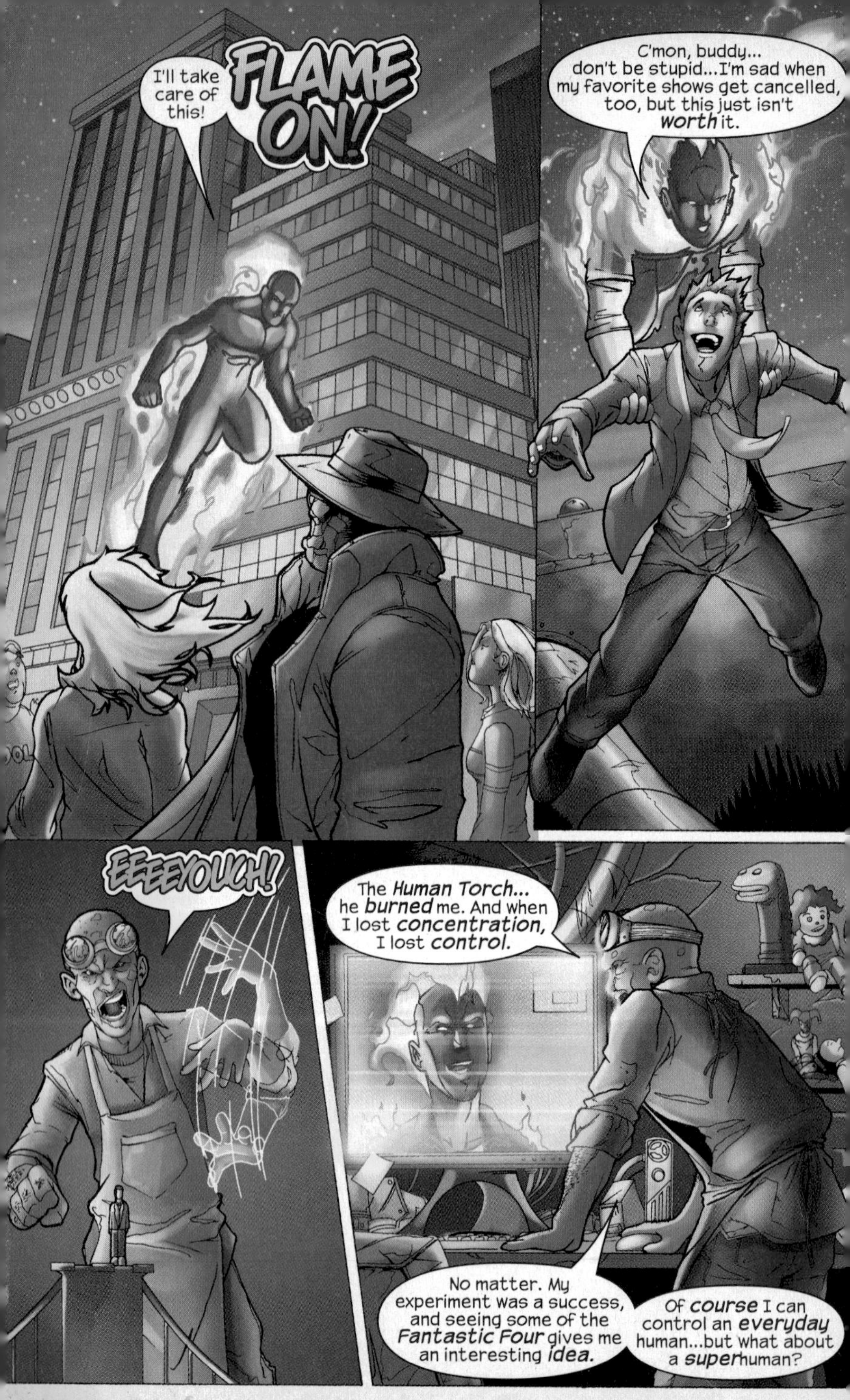
I'll take care of this!
FLAME ON!
C'mon, buddy... don't be stupid...I'm sad when my favorite shows get cancelled, too, but this just isn't worth it.
EEEEYOUCH!
The Human Torch... he burned me. And when I lost concentration, I lost control.
No matter. My experiment was a success, and seeing some of the Fantastic Four gives me an interesting idea.
Of course I can control an everyday human...but what about a superhuman?

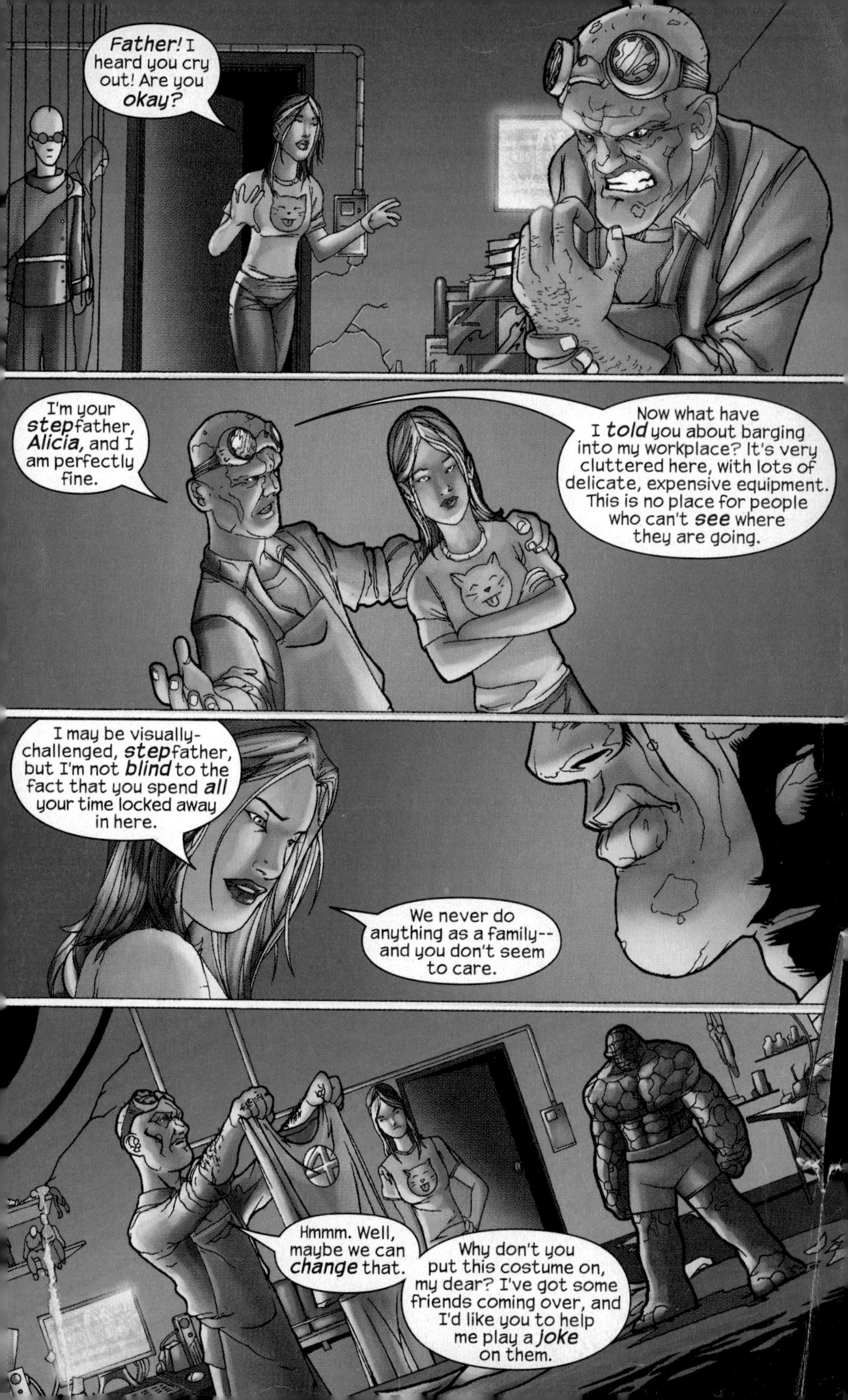
Father! I heard you cry out! Are you okay?
I'm your stepfather, Alicia, and I am perfectly fine.
Now what have I told you about barging into my workplace? It's very cluttered here, with lots of delicate, expensive equipment. This is no place for people who can't see where they are going.
I may be visually-challenged, stepfather, but I'm not blind to the fact that you spend all your time locked away in here.
We never do anything as a family--and you don't seem to care.
Hmmm. Well, maybe we can change that.
Why don't you put this costume on, my dear? I've got some friends coming over, and I'd like you to help me play a joke on them.

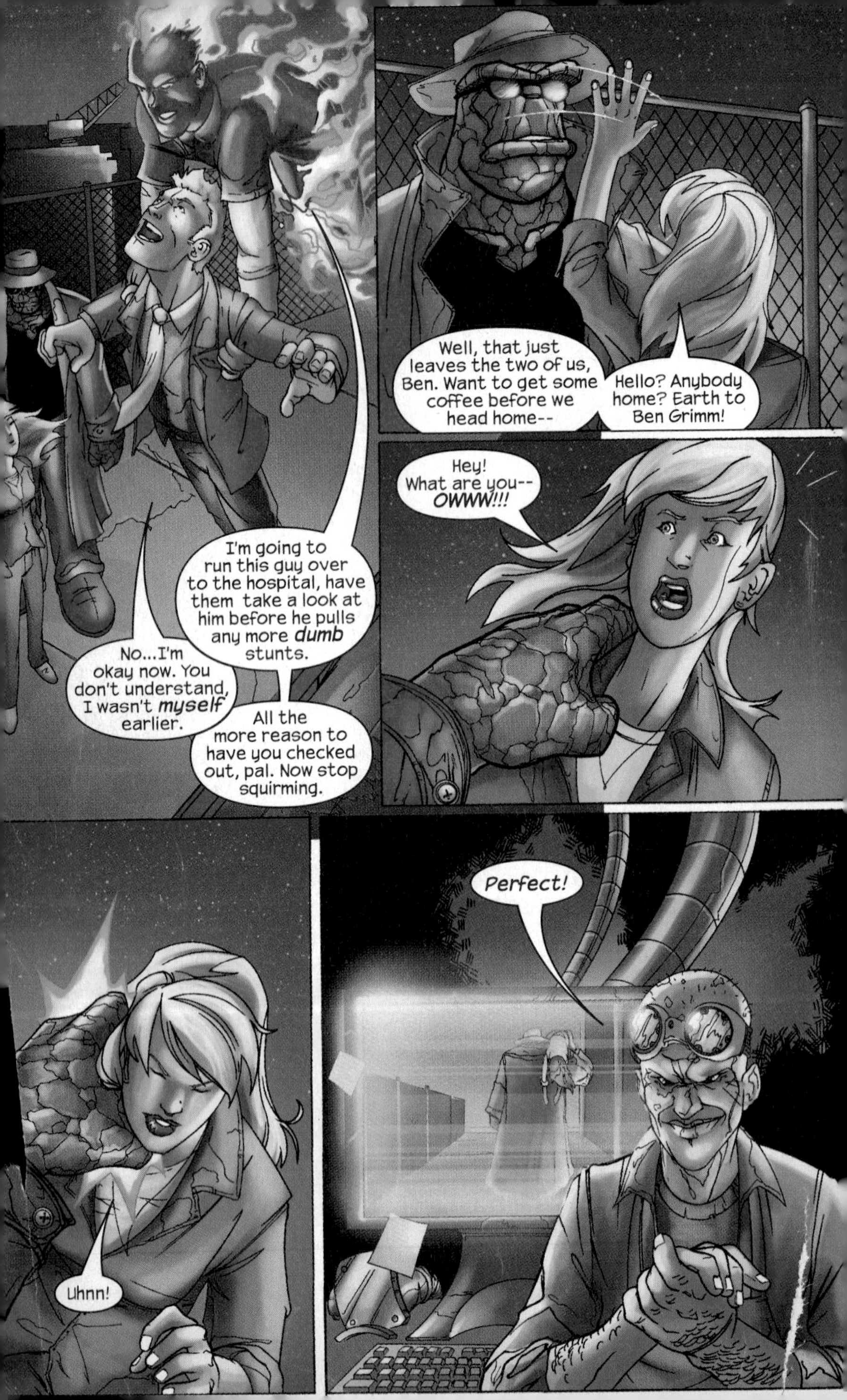
I'm going to run this guy over to the hospital, have them take a look at him before he pulls any more *dumb* stunts.
No...I'm okay now. You don't understand, I wasn't *myself* earlier.
All the more reason to have you checked out, pal. Now stop squirming.
Well, that just leaves the two of us, Ben. Want to get some coffee before we head home--
Hello? Anybody home? Earth to Ben Grimm!
Hey! What are you-- ***OWWW!!!***
Uhnn!
Perfect!

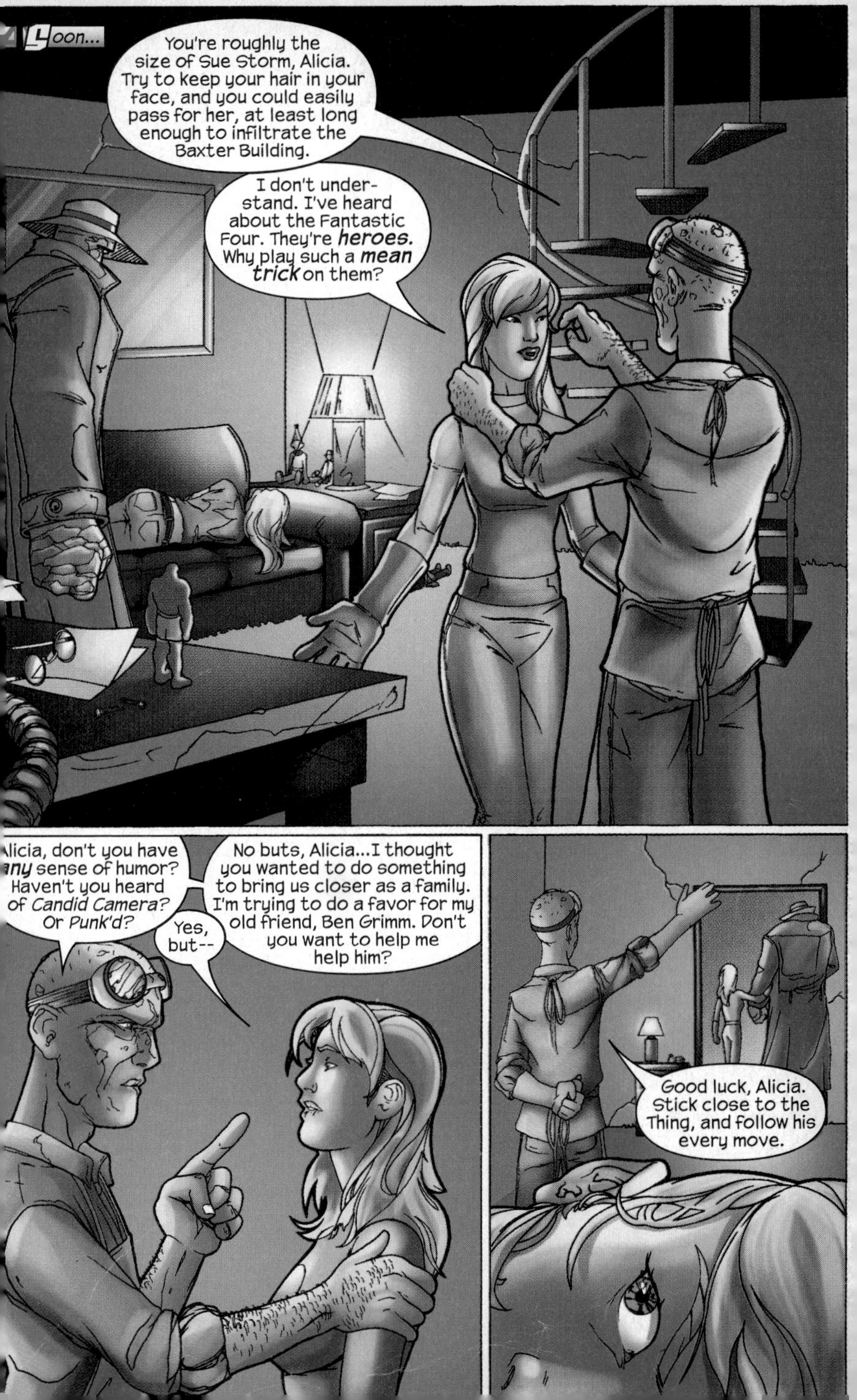

Soon...
You're roughly the size of Sue Storm, Alicia. Try to keep your hair in your face, and you could easily pass for her, at least long enough to infiltrate the Baxter Building.
I don't under-stand. I've heard about the Fantastic Four. They're *heroes.* Why play such a *mean trick* on them?
licia, don't you have *ny* sense of humor? Haven't you heard of *Candid Camera?* Or *Punk'd?*
Yes, but--
No buts, Alicia...I thought you wanted to do something to bring us closer as a family. I'm trying to do a favor for my old friend, Ben Grimm. Don't you want to help me help him?
Good luck, Alicia. Stick close to the Thing, and follow his every move.

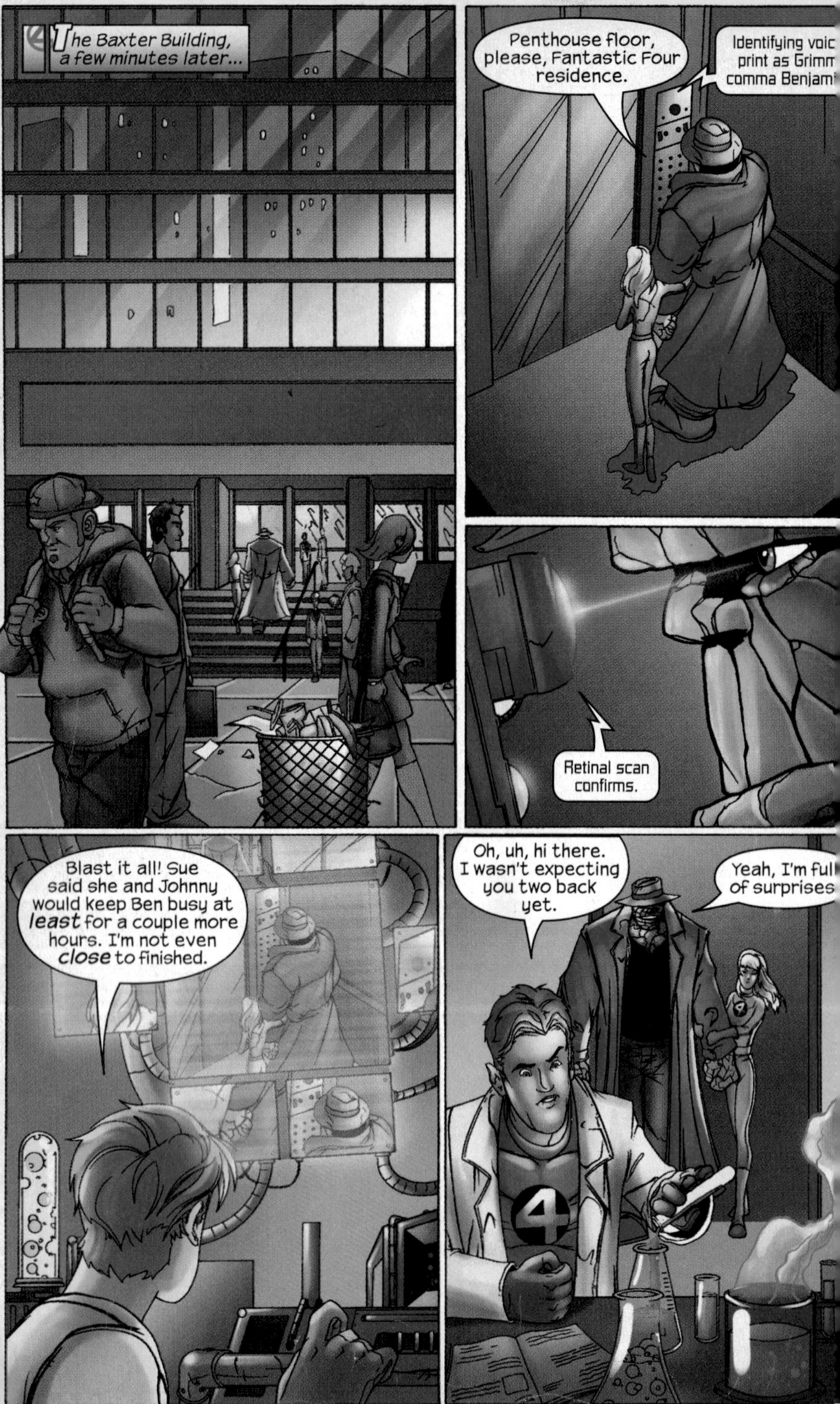
The Baxter Building, a few minutes later...
Penthouse floor, please, Fantastic Four residence.
Identifying voic print as Grimm comma Benjam
Retinal scan confirms.
Blast it all! Sue said she and Johnny would keep Ben busy at *least* for a couple more hours. I'm not even *close* to finished.
Oh, uh, hi there. I wasn't expecting you two back yet.
Yeah, I'm ful of surprises

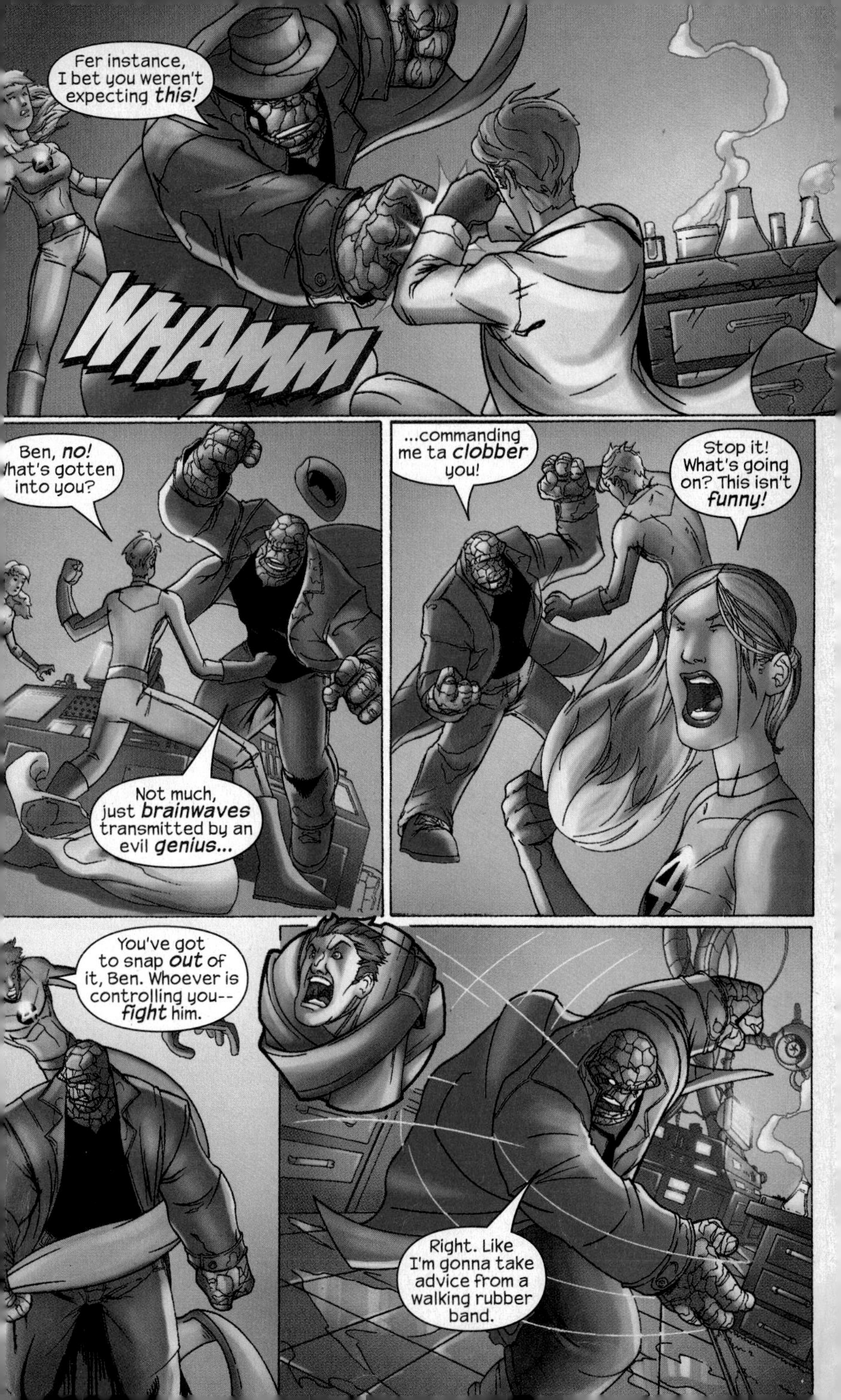
Fer instance, I bet you weren't expecting *this!*
WHAMM
Ben, *no!* What's gotten into you?
Not much, just *brainwaves* transmitted by an evil *genius...*
...commanding me ta *clobber* you!
Stop it! What's going on? This isn't *funny!*
You've got to snap *out* of it, Ben. Whoever is controlling you-- *fight* him.
Right. Like I'm gonna take advice from a walking rubber band.

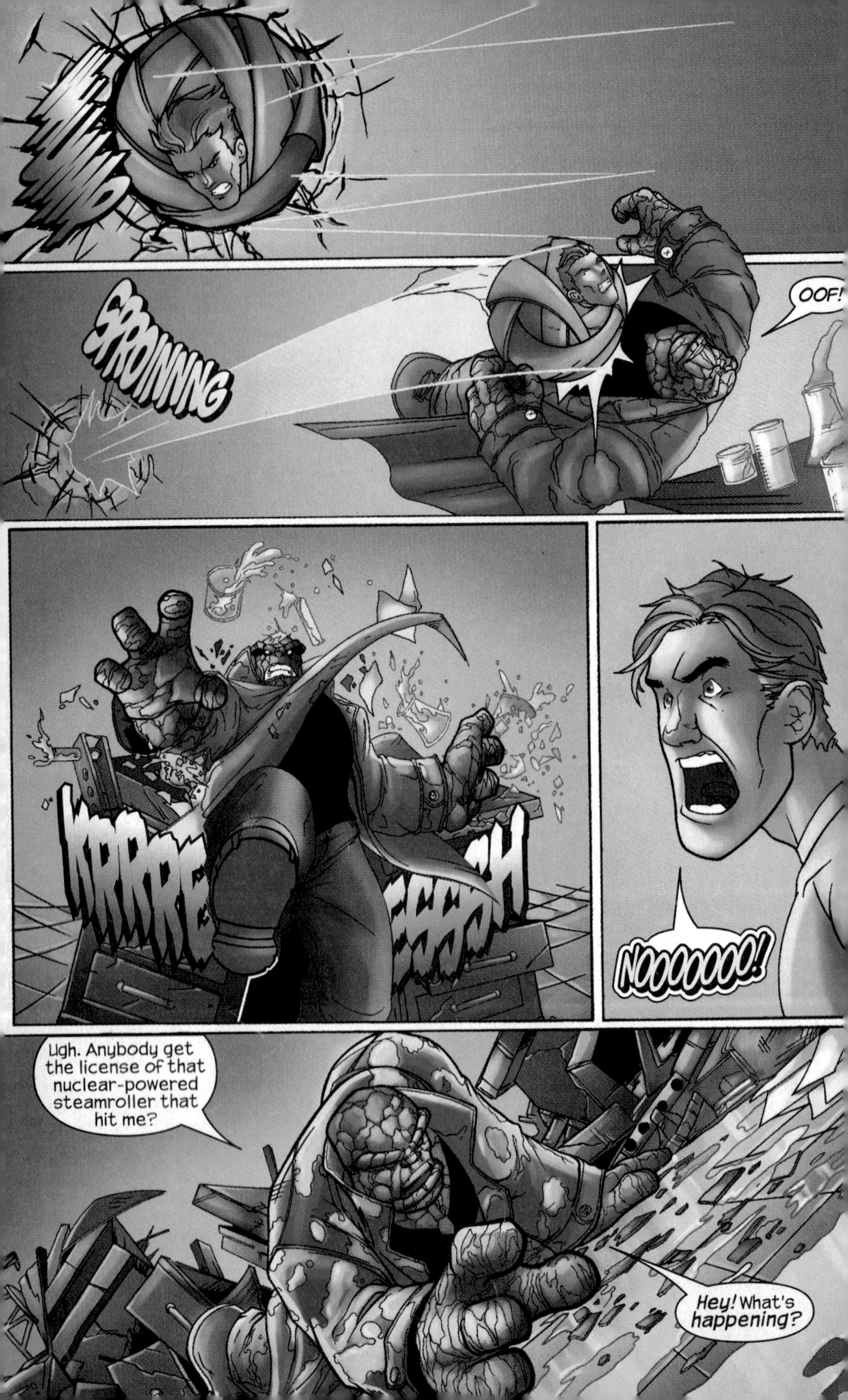
SPROINNNG
OOF!
NOOOOOOO!
Ugh. Anybody get the license of that nuclear-powered steamroller that hit me?
Hey! What's happening?

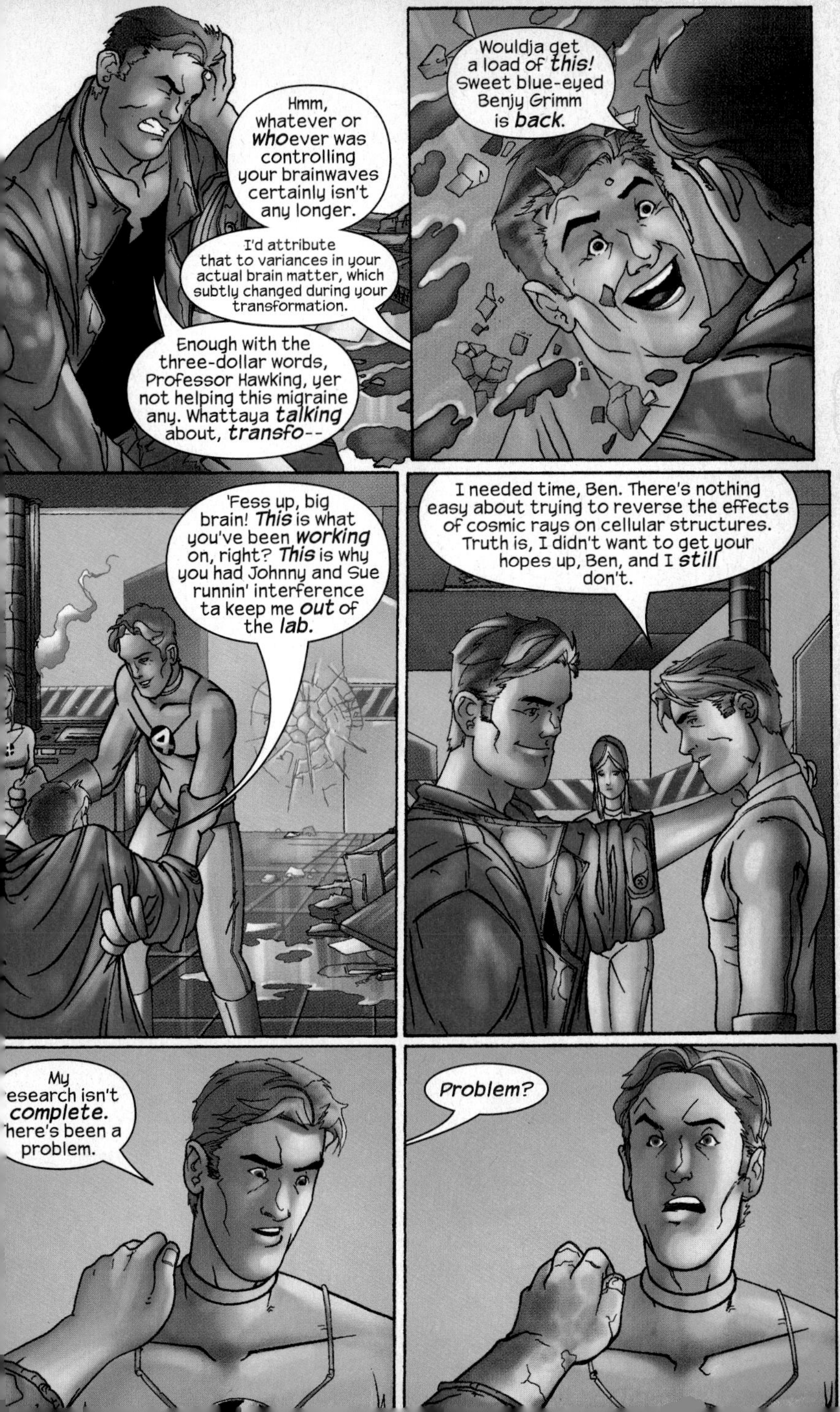
Hmm, whatever or whoever was controlling your brainwaves certainly isn't any longer.
I'd attribute that to variances in your actual brain matter, which subtly changed during your transformation.
Enough with the three-dollar words, Professor Hawking, yer not helping this migraine any. Whattaya talking about, transfo--
Wouldja get a load of this! Sweet blue-eyed Benjy Grimm is back.
'Fess up, big brain! This is what you've been working on, right? This is why you had Johnny and Sue runnin' interference ta keep me out of the lab.
I needed time, Ben. There's nothing easy about trying to reverse the effects of cosmic rays on cellular structures. Truth is, I didn't want to get your hopes up, Ben, and I still don't.
My esearch isn't complete. here's been a problem.
Problem?

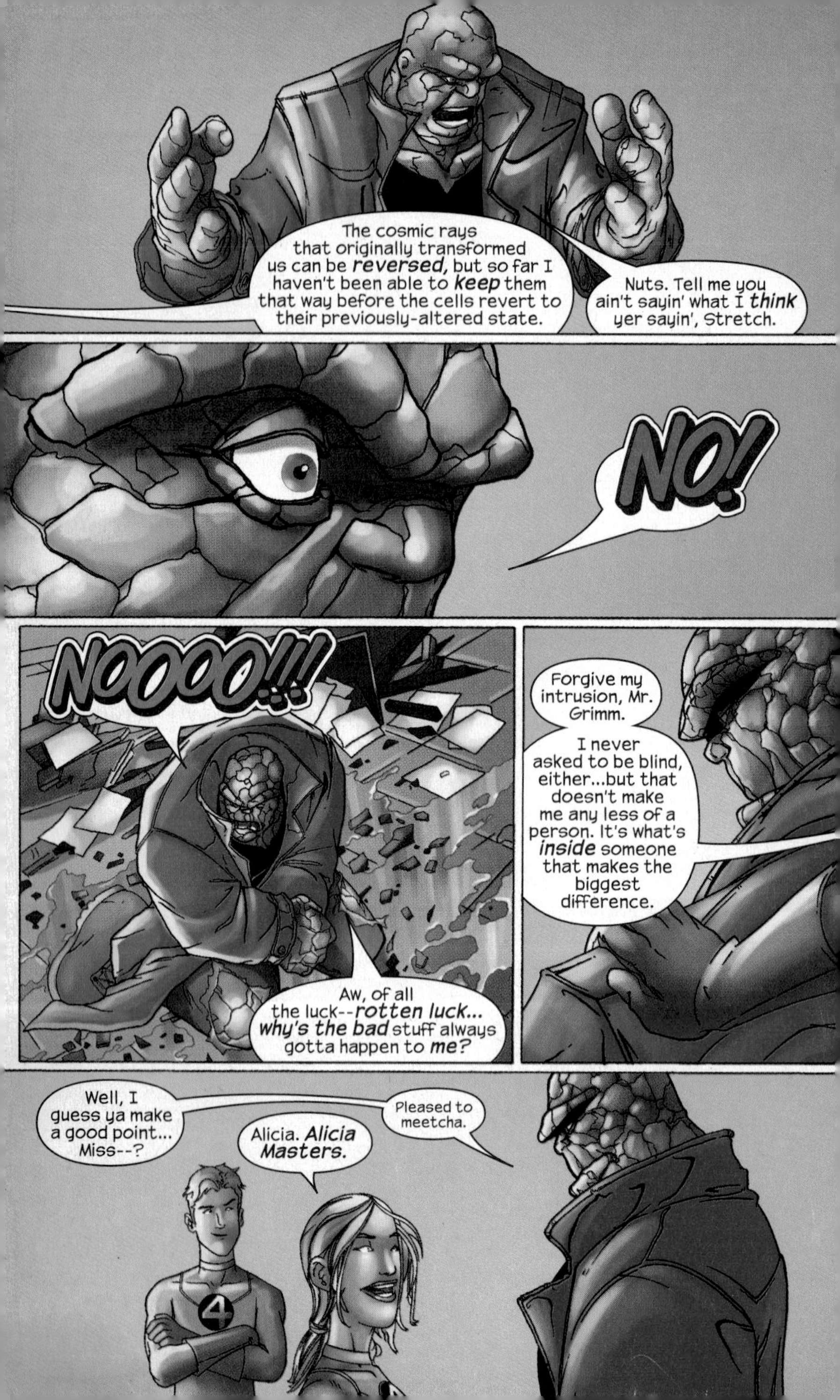
The cosmic rays that originally transformed us can be *reversed,* but so far I haven't been able to *keep* them that way before the cells revert to their previously-altered state.
Nuts. Tell me you ain't sayin' what I *think* yer sayin', Stretch.
NO!
NOOOO!!!
Aw, of all the luck--*rotten luck... why's the bad* stuff always gotta happen to *me?*
Forgive my intrusion, Mr. Grimm.
I never asked to be blind, either...but that doesn't make me any less of a person. It's what's *inside* someone that makes the biggest difference.
Well, I guess ya make a good point... Miss--?
Alicia. *Alicia Masters.*
Pleased to meetcha.

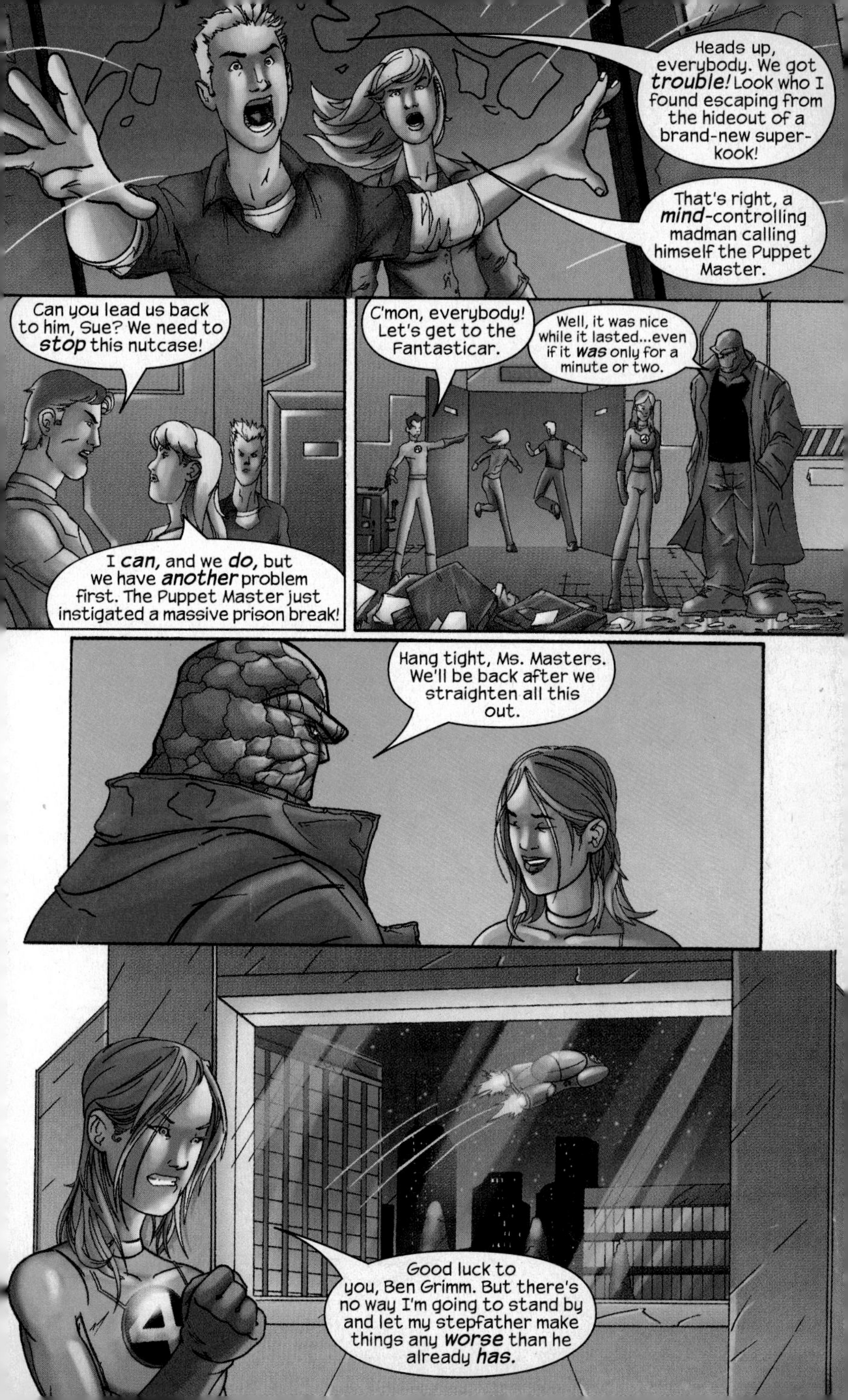

Heads up, everybody. We got *trouble!* Look who I found escaping from the hideout of a brand-new super-kook!
That's right, a *mind*-controlling madman calling himself the Puppet Master.
Can you lead us back to him, Sue? We need to *stop* this nutcase!
I *can,* and we *do,* but we have *another* problem first. The Puppet Master just instigated a massive prison break!
C'mon, everybody! Let's get to the Fantasticar.
Well, it was nice while it lasted...even if it *was* only for a minute or two.
Hang tight, Ms. Masters. We'll be back after we straighten all this out.
Good luck to you, Ben Grimm. But there's no way I'm going to stand by and let my stepfather make things any *worse* than he already *has.*

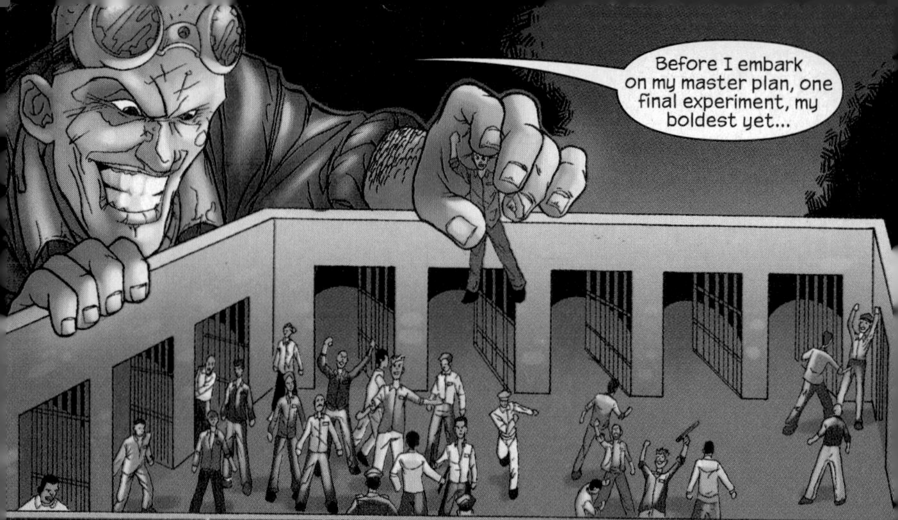
Before I embark on my master plan, one final experiment, my boldest yet...

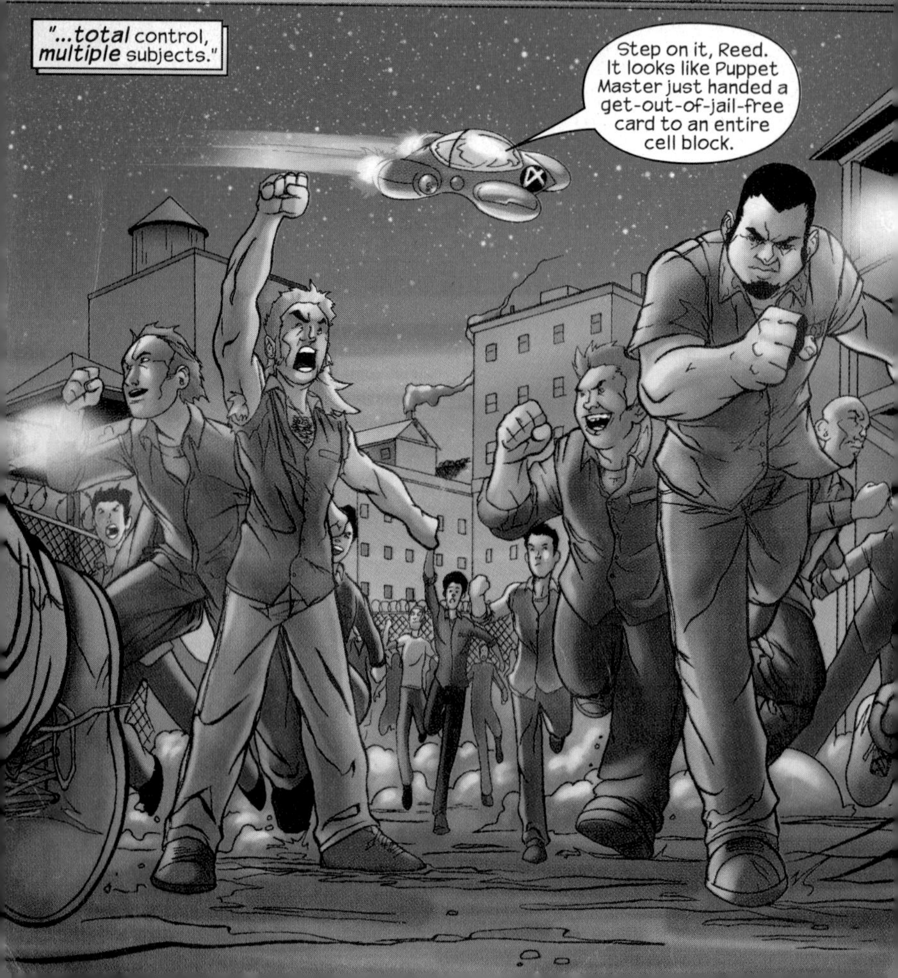
"...*total* control, *multiple* subjects."
Step on it, Reed. It looks like Puppet Master just handed a get-out-of-jail-free card to an entire cell block.

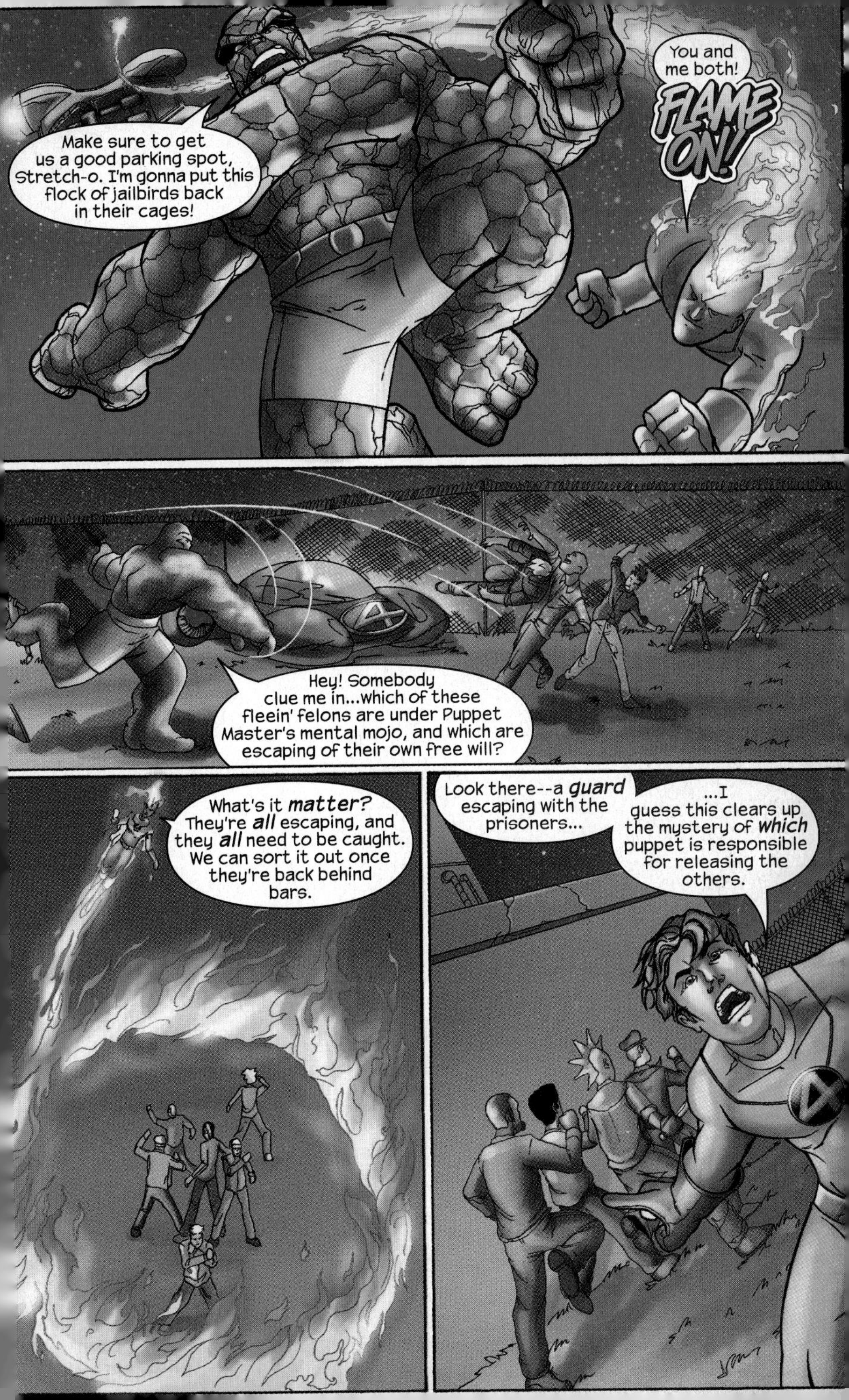
Make sure to get us a good parking spot, Stretch-o. I'm gonna put this flock of jailbirds back in their cages!
You and me both!
FLAME ON!
Hey! Somebody clue me in...which of these fleein' felons are under Puppet Master's mental mojo, and which are escaping of their own free will?
What's it *matter?* They're *all* escaping, and they *all* need to be caught. We can sort it out once they're back behind bars.
Look there--a *guard* escaping with the prisoners...
...I guess this clears up the mystery of *which* puppet is responsible for releasing the others.

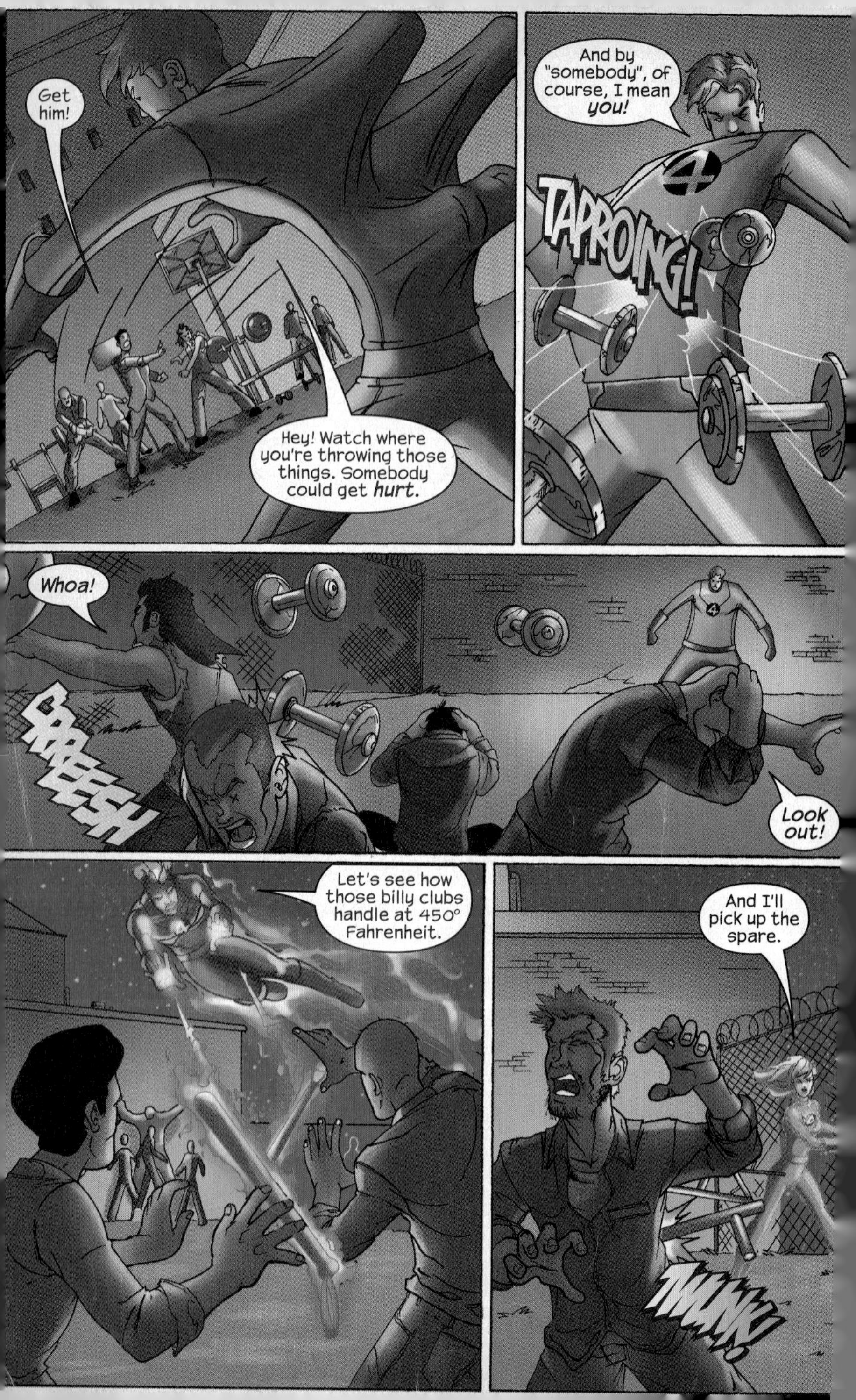
Get him!
Hey! Watch where you're throwing those things. Somebody could get *hurt.*
And by "somebody", of course, I mean *you!*
TAPROING!
Whoa!
CRREESH
Look out!
Let's see how those billy clubs handle at 450° Fahrenheit.
And I'll pick up the spare.
THUNK!

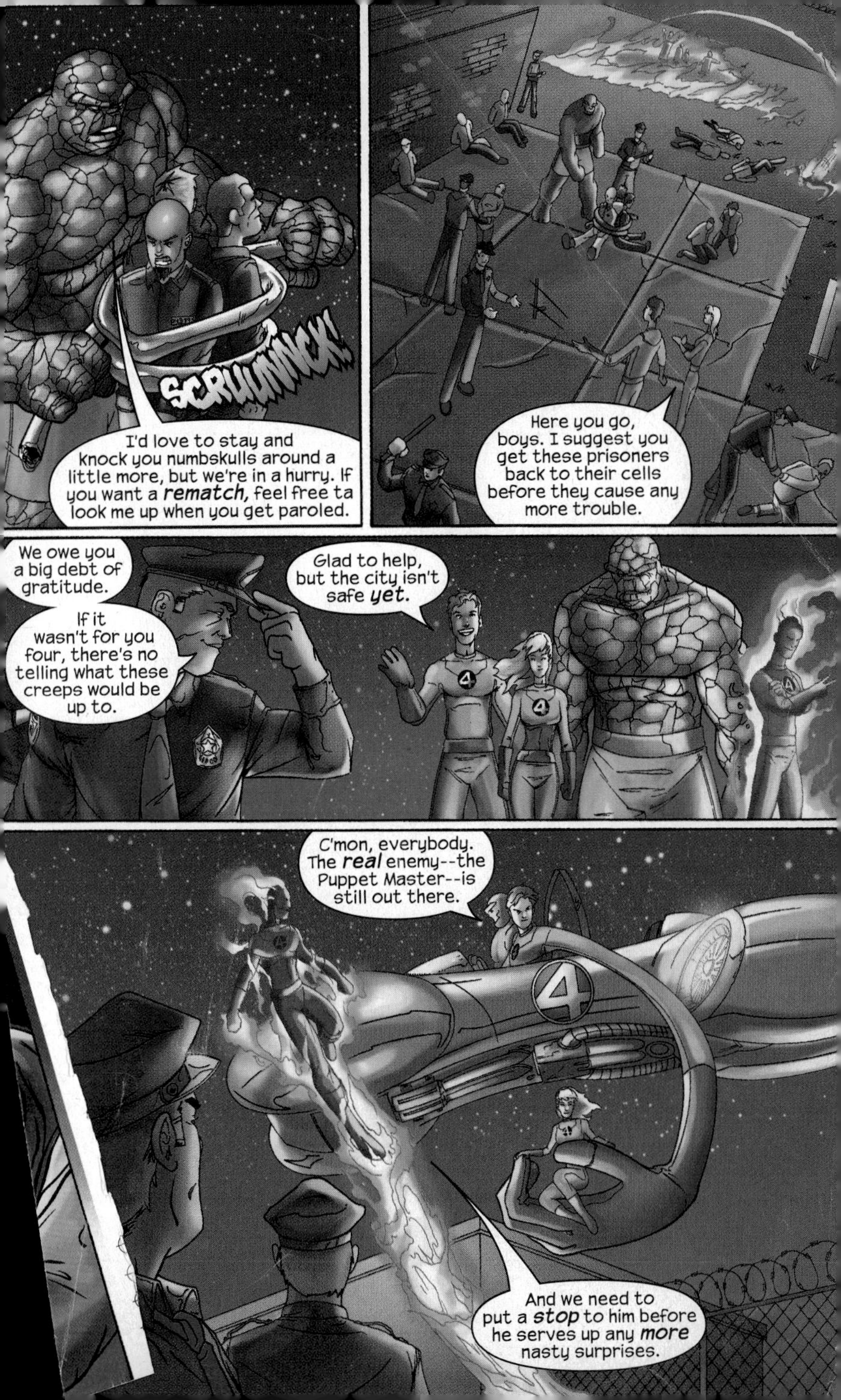
SCRUUNNCK!
I'd love to stay and knock you numbskulls around a little more, but we're in a hurry. If you want a *rematch,* feel free ta look me up when you get paroled.
Here you go, boys. I suggest you get these prisoners back to their cells before they cause any more trouble.
We owe you a big debt of gratitude.
If it wasn't for you four, there's no telling what these creeps would be up to.
Glad to help, but the city isn't safe *yet.*
C'mon, everybody. The *real* enemy--the Puppet Master--is still out there.
And we need to put a *stop* to him before he serves up any *more* nasty surprises.

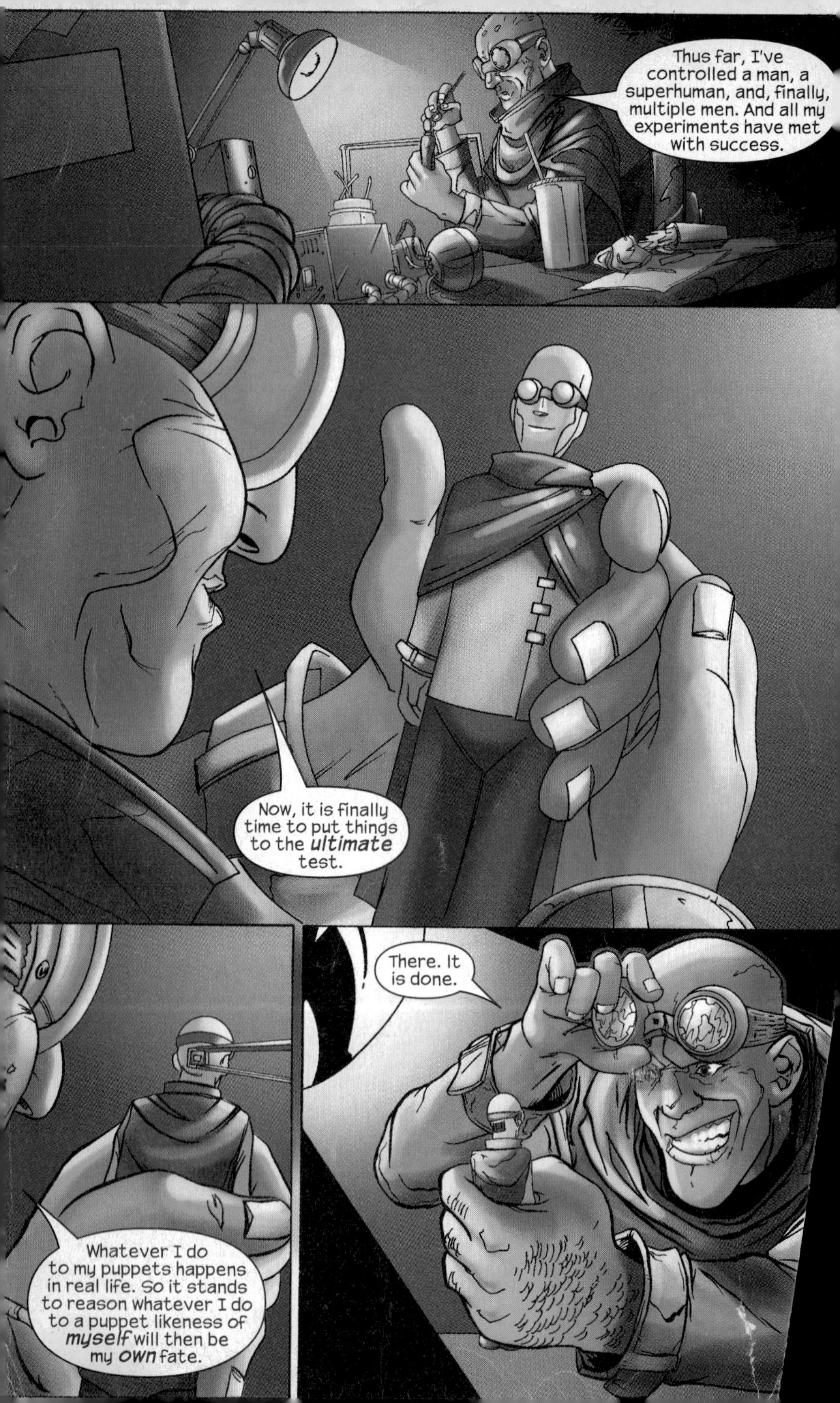

Thus far, I've controlled a man, a superhuman, and, finally, multiple men. And all my experiments have met with success.
Now, it is finally time to put things to the *ultimate* test.
Whatever I do to my puppets happens in real life. So it stands to reason whatever I do to a puppet likeness of *myself* will then be my *own* fate.
There. It is done.

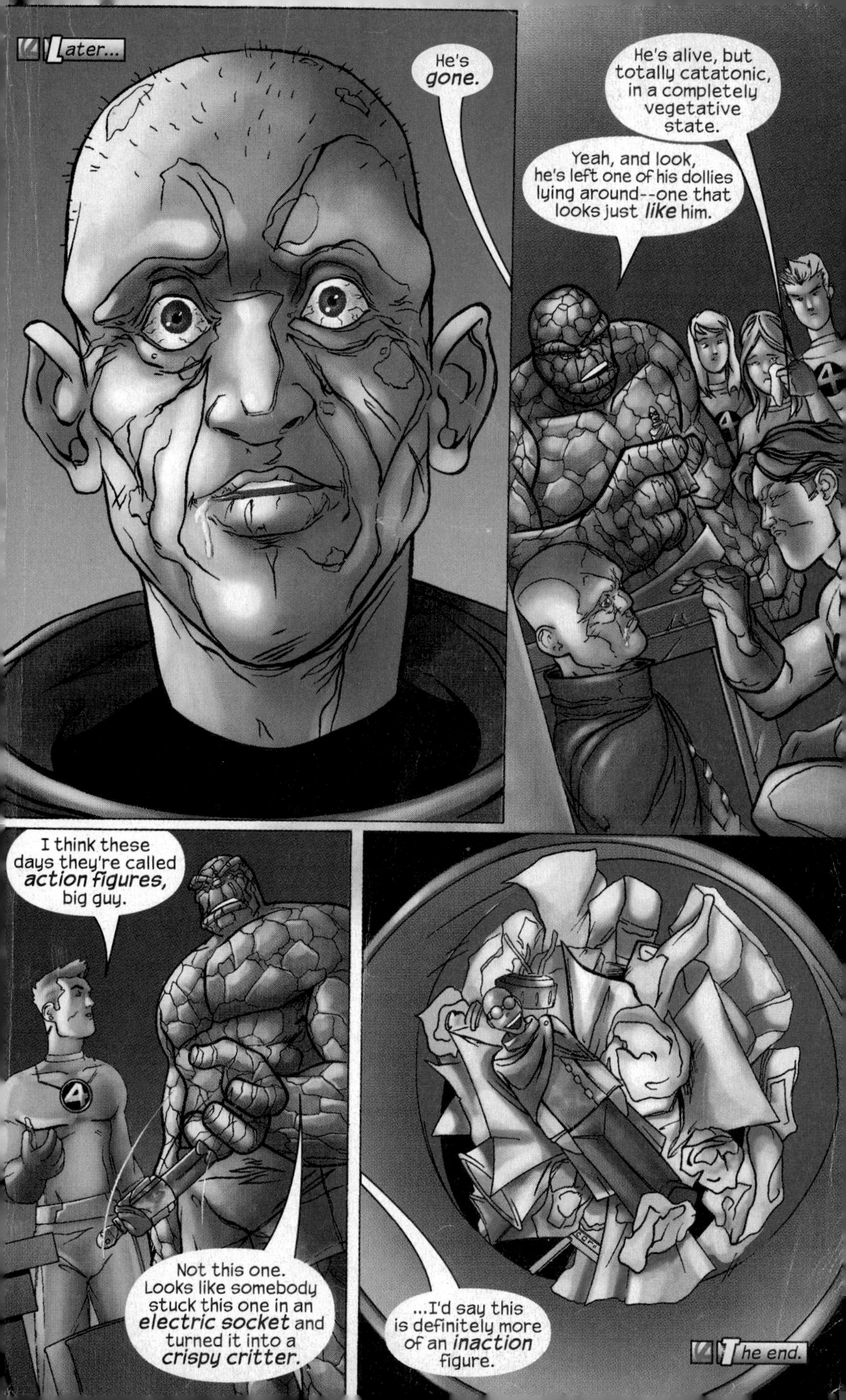
Later...
He's *gone.*
He's alive, but totally catatonic, in a completely vegetative state.
Yeah, and look, he's left one of his dollies lying around--one that looks just *like* him.
I think these days they're called *action figures,* big guy.
Not this one. Looks like somebody stuck this one in an *electric socket* and turned it into a *crispy critter.*
...I'd say this is definitely more of an *inaction* figure.
The end.

MARVEL AGE BACK PAGE

COLLECT ALL THE MARVEL AGE TITLES!

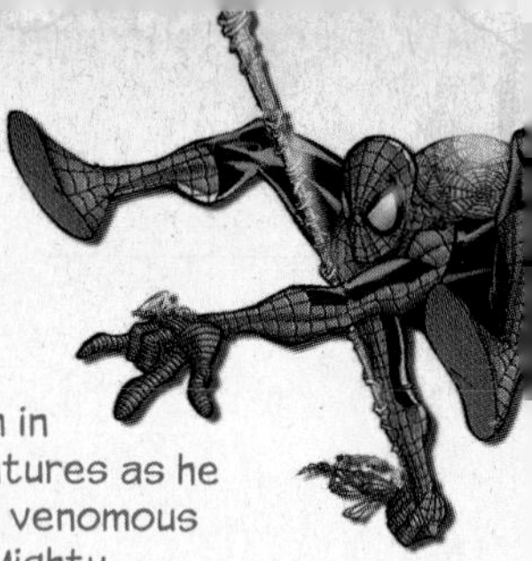

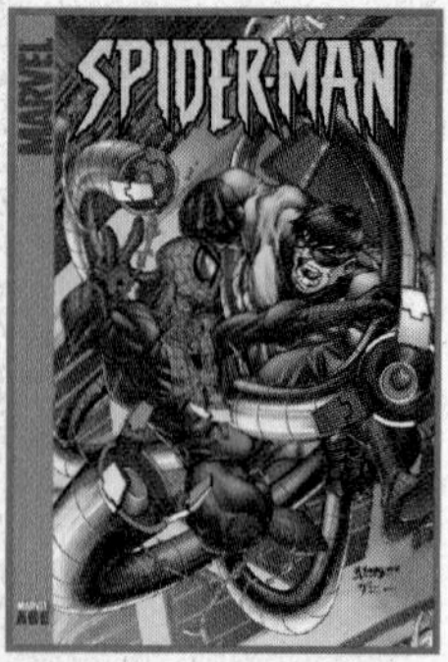
MARVEL
SPIDER-MAN

Catch Spider-Man in his thrilling adventures as he tackles the most venomous villains from the Mighty Marvel Mythos!

- ☐ Marvel Age Spider-Man vol 1 (pictured)
- ☐ Marvel Age Spider-Man vol 2
- ☐ Marvel Age Spider-Man vol 3
- ☐ Marvel Age Spider-Man vol 4

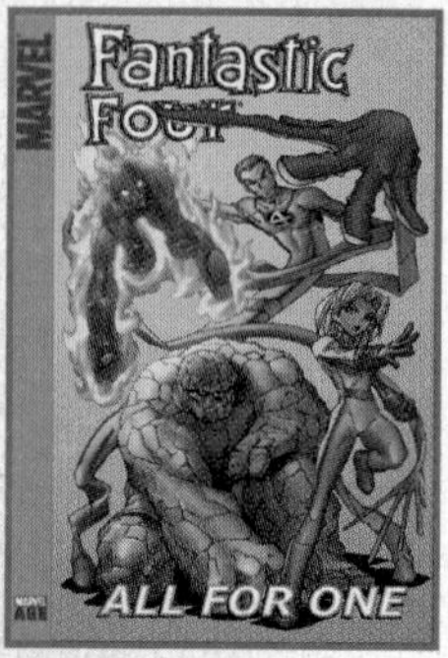
MARVEL
Fantastic Four
ALL FOR ONE

Join Marvel's First Family on their fantastic adventures, from the deepest depths of the ocean to the farthest reaches of outer space!

- ☐ Marvel Age Fantastic Four vol 1 (pictured)
- ☐ Marvel Age Fantastic Four vol 2

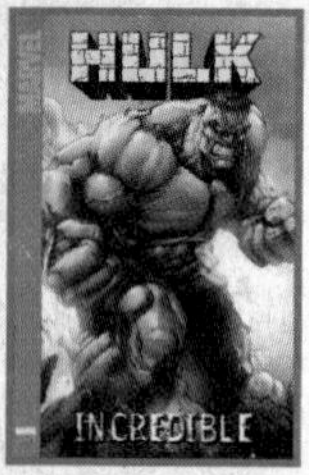
HULK
INCREDIBLE

- ☐ Marvel Age Hulk vol 1: Incredible

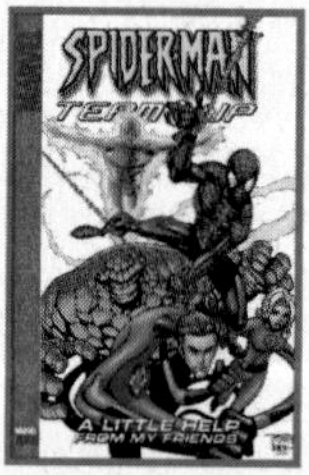
SPIDER-MAN
TEAM-UP
A LITTLE HELP FROM MY FRIENDS

- ☐ Marvel Age Spider-Man Team-Up vol 1: A Little Help From My Friends

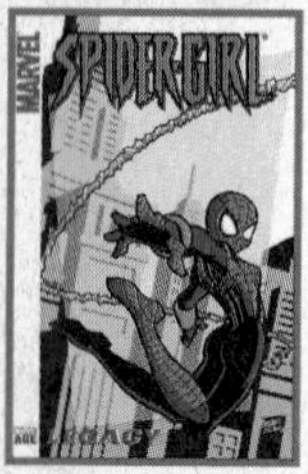
MARVEL
SPIDER-GIRL
LEGACY

- ☐ Marvel Age Spider-Girl vol 1: Legacy (pictured)
- ☐ Marvel Age Spider-Girl vol 2: Like Father Like Daughter

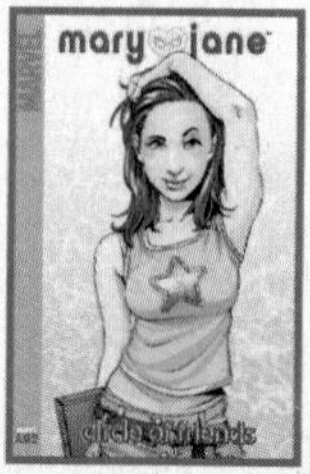
mary jane
circle of friends

- ☐ Marvel Age Mary Jane vol 1: Circle of Friends

Available in bookstores and your local comic shop! Don't miss out!